WHITEHEAD'S

AMERICAN ESSAYS

IN SOCIAL PHILOSOPHY

Whitehead's
American Essays
in Social Philosophy

EDITED

WITH AN INTRODUCTION BY

A. H. JOHNSON
Department of Philosophy
The University of
Western Ontario

GREENWOOD PRESS, PUBLISHERS
WESTPORT, CONNECTICUT

Library of Congress Cataloging in Publication Data

Whitehead, Alfred North, 1861-1947.
    Whitehead's American essays in social philosophy.

    Reprint of the ed. published by Harper, New York.
    Bibliography: p.
    Includes index.
    1. Social sciences--Addresses, essays, lectures.
I. Title.
[H33.W5 1975]   300   74-11997
ISBN 0-8371-7716-2

Originally published in 1959 by Harper & Brothers Publishers,
New York

Reprinted with the permission of A. H. Johnson

Reprinted in 1975 by Greenwood Press,
a division of Williamhouse-Regency Inc.

Library of Congress Catalog Card Number 74-11997

ISBN 0-8371-7716-2

Printed in the United States of America

Contents

v

Preface

Alfred North Whitehead arrived in Cambridge, Massachusetts in 1924, at the age of 63. Already he had acquired an international reputation in the fields of mathematics and the philosophy of science. His careers at Cambridge University and at The University of London were marked not only by brilliant scholarship but also by stimulating teaching and by wise and efficacious administrative activities. He wrote an impressive series of learned volumes: *A Treatise on Universal Algebra; The Axioms of Projective Geometry; The Axioms of Descriptive Geometry;* the three volume *Principia Mathematica* (with Bertrand Russell); *An Introduction to Mathematics; The Organization of Thought; An Enquiry Concerning the Principles of Natural Knowledge; The Concept of Nature; The Principle of Relativity.* There was also a considerable number of technical articles. In addition to all this, Whitehead assumed his responsibilities as a citizen by participating in local politics and by serving on several national "commissions." A wide circle of friends from all walks of life testified to his personal charm and solid worth as a civilized gentleman.

Whitehead found the transition to New England easy and congenial. His American career, begun at a time when most men are getting ready to retire, was in some respects even more impressive than his careers in England. From 1924 to 1937, Whitehead served as professor of philosophy at Harvard. (This was his first professional appointment in philosophy.) During his residence in America he wrote *Science and the Modern World; Religion in the Making; Symbolism, Its Meaning and Effect; Process and Reality; The Function of Reason; Adventure of Ideas;* and *Modes of Thought.* In 1929 there appeared *The Aims of Education and Other Essays.* This is a collection of essays which were, for the most part, originally published in English journals. In America (as in England) he immersed himself in the affairs of his university and the community in general. His home was a gathering place for serious students and also for men eminent in all fields of endeavor.

Incredible as it may seem, it was during this period of intense, highly productive activity that Alfred North Whitehead found time to write a series of essays in social philosophy. These essays constitute one of his great contributions to the culture of our time.* They reveal the balanced sanity of Whitehead's incisive and well-stocked mind. They are characterized by literary excellence. They constitute an effective statement of Whitehead's views on social philosophy.

His discussion of this topic is not confined to the essays reprinted in this volume. There are scattered references to social philosophy in several of his books, in particular *Science and the Modern World* and *Adventures of Ideas.* There is, in addition, his *The Aims of Education.* These books may be regarded as supplementary materials which may add to the appreciation of the essays in this book.

Even a superficial examination of Whitehead's essays in social philosophy reveals his great concern for the values of civiliza-

---

* Some of these essays were later republished in a composite volume entitled *Essays in Science and Philosophy.* One of them was republished as chapter seven of *The Aims of Education.*

tion. In his opinion, societies should be chiefly occupied with the attainment of these ideal values.

It is important, then, to note his definition of civilization, his view concerning the conditions which facilitate its development, and, in general, his theory of the forces and factors which effect human life.

The autobiographic sections of Whitehead's essays are worthy of attention on their own merit. Further, since they deal chiefly with his early life, they are a valuable source of insight into the origins of his social philosophy.

Acknowledgements
Greenwood Press Reprint Edition

In preparing *Whitehead's American Essays in Social Philosophy* for re-issue by the Greenwood Press, I have secured permission from the original publishers to re-use essay material, namely the *Atlantic Monthly,* the *Harvard Business Review, The Andover Bulletin.* This is to record my gratitude. Though the *Radcliffe Quarterly* does not hold copyright on "Historical Changes," I am happy to once again acknowledge this source.

I acknowledge with appreciation permission given by Macmillan Publishing Company, New York, to re-use a number of brief quotations in my introduction—rights covering the United States and Canada.

ADVENTURES OF IDEAS
(Copyright 1933 by Macmillan Publishing Co., Inc., renewed 1961 by Evelyn Whitehead)

THE AIMS OF EDUCATION
(Copyright 1929 by Macmillan Publishing Co., Inc., renewed 1957 by Evelyn Whitehead)

MODES OF THOUGHT
(Copyright 1938 by Macmillan Publishing Co., Inc., renewed 1966 by T. North Whitehead)

PROCESS AND REALITY
(Copyright 1929 by Macmillan Publishing Co., Inc., renewed 1957 by Evelyn Whitehead)

RELIGION IN THE MAKING
(Copyright 1926 by Macmillan Publishing Co., Inc., renewed 1954 by Evelyn Whitehead)

The Cambridge University Press, holder of rights in the world, apart from the United States and Canada, has kindly granted permission to use short passages from the following books by Alfred North Whitehead: *Modes of Thought, Process and Reality, Religion in the Making, Science in the Modern World,* and *Adventures of Ideas.* I am also grateful to Ernest Benn, holder of world rights outside of Canada and the United States for permission to use quotations from *The Aims of Education.*

I wish to express my profound appreciation of the fact that some years ago Professor T. North Whitehead (since deceased) granted me permission to use material published in the writings of Professor Alfred North Whitehead, in so far as it fell within the control of his literary executor.

—A. H. Johnson
May 1974

Acknowledgements

I am deeply grateful to Mrs. Evelyn Whitehead and Professor T. North Whitehead for their very helpful attitude toward this project.

Appreciative acknowledgement is made to the *Atlantic Monthly* for permission to use "An Appeal to Sanity," "England and the Narrow Seas," "Harvard: The Future," "Memories," "The Education of an Englishman," "The Problem of Reconstruction," and "Universities and Their Function;" to the *Harvard Business Review* for permission to use "The Study of the Past—Its Uses and Its Dangers;" to the *Phillips Bulletin* for permission to use "The Importance of Friendly Relations Between England and the United States;" and to the *Radcliffe Quarterly* for permission to use "Historical Changes."

The Macmillan Company of New York has kindly granted permission to quote from the following books by Alfred North Whitehead: *Adventure of Ideas, Modes of Thought, Process and Reality, Religion in the Making, Science and the Modern World,* and *The Aims of Education.* Permission has been given jointly by the Macmillan Company and the *Hibbert Journal* to quote from Chapter 5 of *The Aims of Education.*

The interest and assistance of Mr. Ordway Tead and his associates at Harper and Brothers have been thoroughly appreciated. I wish also to express my gratitude to my colleague, Professor W. Cameron Henry, for assistance in preparing the manuscript;

to Miss Nancy Churchouse for efficient secretarial activities; and to my wife Helen and daughter Sandra who undertook the reading of proof.

A. H. JOHNSON

PART ONE INTRODUCTION

This Introduction to Whitehead's American essays in social philosophy consists of two related sections. The first section is a systematic outline of Whitehead's views concerning civilization. The need for this has been pointed out in the Preface. The second section is an interpretive exposition of the main ideas discussed by Whitehead in his essays in social philosophy. When necessary, reference is made to supplementary material. Both sections include evaluations of Whitehead's ideas.

I

The Meaning of Civilization

THE MEANING OF CIVILIZATION

WITH characteristic honesty, Whitehead admits that the meaning of civilization is obscure. However, he offers as a general definition the suggestion that a civilized society is one which exhibits the following qualities: *truth, beauty, adventure, art,* and *peace*.[1] The full meaning of these terms will be indicated later. It is obvious, even at first glance, that in Whitehead's opinion civilization is primarily concerned with values. Though he does not mention *goodness* in the preceding list, he contends that it is implicit in the other values.

Whitehead states that the values which characterize civilization cannot be developed to the maximum degree unless the rights of individuals are really respected. From this it follows that a civilized society is characterized by tolerance. Persuasion is recognized to be a more effective method of social control than force. Obviously freedom of thought and action are basic prerequisites. These freedoms depend on the acquisition of a trained intelligence. Such an intelligence surveys the world with

[1] See A. N. Whitehead, *Adventures of Ideas* (New York: Macmillan, 1933), p. 353. Hereafter this book will be referred to as *A.I.* (*N.B.* Page notation is the same in the Cambridge University Press edition, 1933.)

an adequate set of generalities, and develops a constructive "critical discontent." The cultivation of these attitudes and abilities will be fostered only if a suitable educational system is established.

The meaning of various "key" terms employed by Whitehead in his discussion of civilization merits careful examination.

ADVENTURE

In introducing his most comprehensive discussion of civilization, Whitehead states that, "adventure is essential . . . [it is] the search for new perfections."[2] It stems from the critical discontent which is aroused when the actual is confronted by the ideal. "A race preserves its vigor so long as it harbours a real contrast between what has been and what may be; and so long as it is nerved by the vigor to adventure beyond the safeties of the past. Without adventure civilization is in full decay."[3] Thus, in a sense, there is a "radical" element in the thinking of Whitehead. He is continually stressing the necessity for change. "Advance or Decadence are the only choices offered to mankind. The pure conservative is fighting against the essence of the Universe."[4] This is not a blind advocacy of change for the sake of change. Rather, it is the search for new perfections. Despite his emphasis on the necessity of adventure, Whitehead does not lose sight of the equal importance of "stability." He reminds us that social life involves a certain amount of routine. These two apparently contrasting emphases are to be regarded as complementary. "The art of progress is to preserve order amid change, and to preserve change amid order."[5]

[2] *A.I.*, p. 332.
[3] *A.I.*, p. 360.
[4] *A.I.*, p. 354.
[5] A. N. Whitehead, *Process and Reality* (New York: Macmillan, 1929), p. 515. Hereafter this book will be referred to as *P.R.*

PEACE

The term "peace" as employed in Whitehead's discussion of civilization has a rich and complex meaning. It is not a state of dreamy relaxation. It does not refer particularly to political or industrial relations. Rather, it is chiefly characterized by calm and penetrating insight into the status of values and the true worth of individuals. "Its first effect is the removal of the stress of acquisitive feeling arising from the soul's pre-occupation with itself." It is "a quality of mind steady in its reliance that fine action is treasured in the nature of things."[6] When peace is present in the mind of a civilized man, the distractions of fame and fortune, the gnawing worries which spring from narrow egoism, lose their power. In other words, the man who loses himself in the pursuit of the great things of life is no longer distracted by the little things. He can see good and evil in their true perspective. He is convinced that what is worthwhile is not in vain.

ART

In Whitehead's opinion, a work of art is a way of expressing the truth about the nature of things. This, however, is only one of its functions. It is also an attempt to express beauty. A superior work of art fuses these two functions. The value of art in the life of a civilized man lies in the fact that it emphasizes that human beings can achieve a degree of perfection, can rise above the pressure of immediate animal needs. The beauty of a mountain range brings to man an overwhelming sense of his littleness. On the other hand, the beauty of a work of art is an exhilarating symbol of the power of human creativity. There is a further value in art. Vivid experiences are relived, free from the relentless pressure of on-going events. For example, the glow of the

[6] *A.I.*, pp. 367, 353.

sunset, which in the physical world lasts for only a minute, can be enjoyed for hours in the realm of aesthetic experience as one stands before a great painting. Finally, great art stresses the importance of individual components as essential elements in the unified group to which they belong. For instance, in the cathedral at Chartes the details of the symbolic carvings stand out as inescapably individual items, yet all contribute to the integrated beauty of the Gothic masterpiece.

TRUTH AND BEAUTY

In his general definition of civilization, Whitehead mentions truth and beauty in addition to adventure, peace, and art. His technical discussion of these terms need not be considered here. Briefly, truth is the correspondence of the symbol with the object symbolized—for example, when a table is called square, as a matter of fact it is square. Beauty, in its highest form is characterized, as is the case in the complex structure of a great symphony, by patterned contrast. Ultimately Whitehead takes the position of Platonism and claims that objects are beautiful when they manifest the "ideal" Beauty; statements (and other symbols) are true when they manifest the "ideal" Truth.

REQUISITES FOR CIVILIZED LIVING

As has been noted, Whitehead contends that the distinctive values that characterize civilization can be fully achieved only in a society of a specific sort. This point requires elaboration.

PROPER EVALUATION OF INDIVIDUALS

His emphasis on the importance and value of the individual leads him to oppose all forms of social organization which tend to stunt the legitimate development of the individual. "The worth of any social system depends on the value experience it promotes among individual human beings. . . . If the man be wholly subordinated to the common life, he is dwarfed."[7] Whitehead is prepared to admit that exceptional behavior may be foolish, but he stresses the fact that some eccentric behavior may be "beyond price."

TOLERANCE

In a civilized society, mere toleration (if by that one means non-interference) is not enough. There must be genuine respect (real *tolerance*) for one's fellow men everywhere. "It cannot be repeated too often that the only security for progress is a sincere respect for each individual human being."[8] Thus in the area of international relations, it is important to remember that "a diversification among human communities is essential for the provision of the incentive and material for the Odyssey of the human spirit."[9]

With characteristic keen insight, Whitehead sets the problem of tolerance in a comprehensive context. He suggests, for example, that we should be tolerant because we human beings labor under definite limitations. The complexity of the past and present cannot be grasped by our finite minds. The novelty of the future is quite beyond our understanding. Hence, the only honest attitude is the avoidance of dogmatism. In an interesting aside he notes that tolerance is not frequently found in "advanced" thinkers. It is more likely to appear in a social environment marked by "genial orthodoxy." Great reformers (e.g., Calvin)

[7] "An Appeal to Sanity," pp. 124–125 this volume.
[8] "The Problem of Reconstruction," pp. 55–56 this volume.
[9] A. N. Whitehead, *Science and the Modern World* (New York: Macmillan, 1929), p. 298. Hereafter this book will be referred to as *S.M.W.* (Whitehead expresses the same idea in more pungent form thus: "Sheer contempt betokens blindness." *P.R.*, p. 513.)

are frequently extremely intolerant in their dealings with their enemies, particularly when they (the reformers) assume power. On the other hand men like Erasmus, secure in their conviction of mature wisdom, can afford to smile at the "foibles" of others.

PERSUASION

One of Whitehead's comments on civilization makes the point that "civilization is the maintenance of social order, by its own inherent persuasiveness as embodying the nobler alternative." He clarifies his meaning and brings out a related insight in the remark, "the recourse to force, however unavoidable, is a disclosure of the failure of civilization."[10]

Offhand it seems naive to assign any efficacy to "rational persuasion" in international relations in this ruthless twentieth century world. It is all very well to denounce force, but force is the most effective agency for getting things done—this is the obvious criticism of Whitehead's position. Yet, despite this, he sincerely advocates the use of persuasion, based on free discussion, leading to a mutually acceptable solution. He notes that in 1931 Ghandi and the Viceroy of India achieved at least a temporary solution of a complex social problem by rational discussion rather than by force. Again, India in its transition from British colony to independent nation in 1947 illustrates the efficacy of the same principle. Perhaps it is a childish simplification of a complex situation to claim that persuasion frequently works on the international stage in this day and age. However the present cooperation of the U.S.A. and the members of the British Commonwealth of Nations seems to illustrate further the efficacy of this technique. Rational persuasion does not always "work easily." Whitehead's point is that it is a practical principle of procedure.

[10] *A.I.*, p. 105.

In any case, when persuasion is replaced by force, civilization is in decline.

FREEDOM

Whitehead's advocacy of the importance of the individual and the related emphasis on tolerance indicates his opposition to totalitarianism and "exclusive" nationalism. However, he is not an advocate of unqualified individualism. He contends that it is nonsense to speak of absolute individuals with absolute rights. In his opinion, this is evident because each human being depends on his environment at every moment of his existence. Further, Whitehead agrees with those who claim that rights are relative to the total situation and that they also involve a reference to correlative duties. Whitehead summarizes his position by suggesting that there must be a mingling of individual liberty and environmental compulsion. Unqualified liberty and dull standardization are evils which are equally obnoxious. In attempting to make his point as specific as possible, Whitehead refers to Athens in the days of Pericles (as described by Thucydides).[11] In other words, he suggests that the individual freedom one can expect within a social group is a limited freedom, limited so as to avoid the destruction of the general purpose of the society.

Whitehead offers the interesting suggestion that one way to deal with the problem of freedom and compulsion, in certain

11 It should be recalled that this was a social system where (a) laws afford equal justice to all citizens; (b) advancement, among citizens, depends on proven ability; (c) a person is free to do what he likes; however, he will be controlled by respect for laws, both written and unwritten; (d) administration is in the hands of the many rather than the few; (e) a high level of moral behavior is required from a citizen; (f) if a man advocates a line of public policy, persuades his fellow citizens to accept it, and the results are disastrous, he should be fined, lose his citizenship, or be put to death. It is, of course, obvious that Whitehead would not support Pericles' denial of citizenship to women, manual laborers, foreigners, and slaves.

spheres of human activity, is to vest the control of the individual not in the state but in the professional group to which he belongs. The control which these professional groups should exercise involves an examination of the skills possessed by members of the group. This does not mean complete control of all phases of life. There is room for wide differences of opinion in non-professional areas and also in the details of professional practice. But, to repeat, with respect to his professional field a man's ability is most carefully examined. His status and privileges are then determined. For example, a medical doctor will be examined by other medical doctors as to his professional competence. No control will be exercised over his recreations or political or religious beliefs unless they unmistakably undermine his efficacy as a practitioner. It should be noted also that a professional group can exercise a certain amount of control over non-members of the group by evaluating, for the information of the general public, ideas and actions which fall within the scope of their professional field.

Despite his suggestion concerning the function of professional groups in providing a proper mixture of freedom and compulsion, Whitehead is clearly aware of one serious deficiency in modern professional life. He feels that in the modern world many intellectuals are suffering from a stultifying narrowness of outlook. They specialize in one restricted sphere of interest. Any other area of knowledge, or action, is regarded as unimportant and dealt with, if at all, in terms of their major interest. This frequently leads to a misunderstanding of what is involved in the total situation. For example, some mathematicians are so impressed by the clarity of their abstract systems that they do not understand the complexities and obscurities of ordinary social living. As a result they make a poor adjustment to their social environment. Following this all too accurate description of many modern "wise men," Whitehead offers the trenchant comment that the coordination of the work of specialists often is left to men unable to qualify as specialists. Thus the blind lead the one-eyed.

EDUCATION

Whitehead is convinced that these deficiencies can be overcome, and the requirements of civilized living met, through the medium of an adequate system of education. This should provide a thorough knowledge of one's self, and also of one's physical and social environment. It would serve to enlighten a receptive mind concerning human powers and limitations. In addition to these obvious values, adequate education conveys a philosophic outlook. The meaning of the phrase "philosophic outlook" is indicated by the following statement: "In philosophy, the fact, the theory, the alternatives, and the ideal, are weighed together. Its gifts are insight and foresight, and a sense of the worth of life; in short, the sense of importance which nerves all civilized effort."[12]

It is Whitehead's opinion that aesthetic experience is important as a source of stimulation and discipline. For example: "Great art is the arrangement of the environment so as to provide for the soul vivid, but transient, values. . . . Great art is more than a transient refreshment. It is something which adds to the permanent richness of the soul's self-attainment."[13] In referring to the educational value of art, Whitehead does not intend to distract attention from other types of value. As he himself points out, "What is wanted is an appreciation of the infinite variety of

12 *A.I.*, p. 125.
13 *S.M.W.*, pp. 290–291.

vivid values achieved by an organism in its proper environment."[14]

DECISIVE SOCIAL FACTORS

Whitehead states that there are four factors which decisively govern the fate of social groups. This analysis refers to (a) the influence of *ideas,* (b) the importance of *economic activities* for the satisfaction of human needs, (c) the efficacy of *great men,* and (d) the impact of the *inanimate world.*

One of the great values of Whitehead's social philosophy is its comprehensive sanity. He refuses to assign supreme initiative to any one factor. He tries to examine all the chief ones and to recognize their relative importance.

IDEAS

The references to "transcendent aim" and "trained intelligence" indicate the importance which Whitehead assigns to ideas as efficacious factors in shaping the course of human affairs. He claims that in any era there is a set of ideas, so pervasive of its texture of life that it is accepted as naturally as the air we breathe. For example, throughout the Hellenic-Roman period slavery was regarded as a natural and inescapable fact. Attempts at reform foundered on the rock of this firmly established idea. In discussing the idea of the "intellectual and moral grandeur of the human soul" he indicates how this idea (ideal) gradually was formulated and developed by Plato, the Stoics, Hebrew prophets, and early Christians. It later received specific expression in legal, political, ethical, and religious forms. It then began to function as "a hidden driving force, haunting humanity, and ever appearing in specialized guise as compulsory on action by

[14] *S.M.W.,* p. 286.

reason of its appeal to the uneasy conscience of the age."[15] The tremendous efficacy of scientific ideas is sketched in detail in *Science and the Modern World* and stressed in other relevant discussions of social philosophy.

In discussing the efficacy of ideas, Whitehead is careful to show that ideas are not always immediately effective. As has been noted, the idea of human worth and dignity lured men for centuries before it finally produced concrete results in economic and political behavior. Thus it must be admitted by those who stress the initiative of thought that it is sometimes necessary to take a long range view. Many centuries elapsed between the preaching of Hebrew prophets concerning the dignity of man and the freeing of slaves in America.

Whitehead is also well aware of the fact that ideas may restrict action as well as stimulate it. "A civilization which cannot burst through its current abstractions is doomed to sterility after a very limited period of progress."[16] For example, a scheme of thought may be useful in guiding observation and explaining facts. However, there is always the danger that a system of thought may blind one to some facts and lead one to misinterpret others—for example, the medieval theory that the earth is the center of the universe.

In considering the effect of food and clothing and the activities of commerce (and in general the solving of immediate practical problems), Whitehead seems to contradict his emphasis on the importance of ideas. He states, "Such activities, energizing for centuries, . . . lie behind the intellectual ferment which we find driving onward the Hebrew prophets and the Greek philosophers."[17] Yet in the last analysis, Whitehead seems to hold that

[15] *A.I.*, p. 19.
[16] *S.M.W.*, p. 86.
[17] *A.I.*, p. 88.

the way people react to these material factors is determined by their basic beliefs. Thus he remarks, "As we think, we live. This is why the assemblage of philosophical ideas . . . moulds our type of civilization."[18] In other words, men do not merely adjust passively to these material factors. There is active adaptation. One must have a physical environment, of course, but its nature can be changed. Further, even though, in some cases, the material environment cannot be changed, one's reactions to it may take various forms.

Ideas are expressed by words or other symbols. Whitehead emphasizes the function of symbolism in society. Language is important since it serves to arouse and focus instincts and emotions, which with habits and prejudices are very important ingredients in the social life of man. Further, language facilitates freedom of thought and the creative "criticism" which are of the essence of civilization. Just as ideas may in some cases interfere with progress, so also may symbols. Here, as elsewhere, Whitehead emphasizes the inescapable fact of change. For example, a mathematical system which can not do justice to minute differences is a block to progress and in due course is replaced, or at least supplemented.

MEN

Among the basic factors which shape the course of human history are great men. (a) They introduce the basic ideas of a civilization, ideas which gradually increase their influence by seeping down to lesser men. (b) They serve as symbols around which a nation unites. (c) Finally, their deeds inspire others to imitate them, and hence act as a spur to general advance.

[18] A. N. Whitehead, *Modes of Thought* (New York: Macmillan, 1938), p. 87. Hereafter this book will be referred to as *M.T.*

The immense influence which may be wielded by a few men is carefully noted. For example, Whitehead claims that The Hebrew prophets, Socrates, Jesus, Galileo, and Newton exerted a decisive influence. Further, he suggests that English social history in the nineteenth century cannot be understood unless one is aware of the powerful impact of a relatively few men—chiefly clergymen and aristocrats of liberal opinion.

Whitehead is concerned with the efficacy of "men with ideas." This, however, does not mean that he is oblivious to the influence of "men with the mailed fist." He points out, for instance, that the Byzantine armies under Belisarius and Narses cleared Italy from Gothic domination. This was one of the factors which made possible the subsequent flowering of civilization in that area. Whitehead's judgment on the relative importance of these two types of great men is expressed vigorously in the concluding paragraph of *Science and the Modern World*. "The great conquerors, from Alexander . . . to Napoleon, influenced profoundly the lives of subsequent generations. But the total effect of this influence shrinks to insignificance, if compared to the entire transformation of human habits and human mentality produced by the long line of men of thought . . . men individually powerless, but ultimately the rulers of the world."[19]

However, great men are not irresistible. He notes that such men cannot lead their people into "the promised land" unless they are willing to be led. In other words, a great man is instrumental in bringing about the realization of an ideal only if that ideal has taken sufficient hold of the imaginations and beliefs of men, so that they understand what he is talking about and consider the plan to be sufficiently worthwhile to implement. However, human prejudices, or laziness, are not the only factors

[19] *S.M.W.*, p. 300.

which interfere with the realization of ideals. The situation may be so complex that the existence of a large number of men of good will is not sufficient to bring about the reforms under consideration. For instance, sometimes the economic and social structure is such that sweeping reforms cannot be immediately instigated without running the risk of destroying the possibility of all social life. It is the old problem of "means and end." Sometimes the achievement of a good goal involves the use of evil means, means so evil that the end will be corrupted. In that case it seems better to endure a lesser evil rather than set up a greater one. Whitehead suggests the possibility that the continuation of slavery was justified for a time, since it made possible the preservation of the Hellenic-Roman culture. Further advice is offered to reformers. He counsels them not to trust in some *one* abstract plan for world wide social reconstruction. The complexity of human affairs is such that adjustments must be made— compromise must be accepted. There is also the somewhat ironic comment, "We cannot be social reformers all the time. In our off moments we view our peculiar domestic mixture of goods and evils with an affectionate tolerance of their incongruities, which we call 'humor.' "[20]

Whitehead refers to the importance of ideas formulated in the early years of the Christian era, and that suggests that some religious leaders have exerted a decisive influence. This brings to mind the problem of the function of religion in civilization. In general, Whitehead suggests that "though religion can be a source of progress, it need not be so."[21] For example, the Methodists produced the final effective force which made slavery im-

[20] "The Education of an Englishman," p. 144 this volume.
[21] A. N. Whitehead, *Religion in the Making* (New York: Macmillan, 1926), p. 28. Hereafter this book will be referred to as *R.M.*

possible. Of course, Quakers, Catholics, and other groups (religious and secular) contributed to the common cause. Yet the history of religion does not present a clear record in this matter. "History, . . . is a melancholy record of the horrors which can attend religion: human sacrifice, . . . abject superstition, . . . hysteria, bigotry, can all be laid at its charge. Religion is the last refuge of human savagery."[22] This, however, is not Whitehead's final word on the topic of religion. Rather, one of the most impressive themes in *Adventures of Ideas, Science and the Modern World, Process and Reality,* and *Religion in the Making* is Whitehead's outline and defense of a suggested "New Reformation" which should come to purify religion of its diseases. This topic is too extensive to be dealt with in this introductory essay.[23]

MATERIAL FACTORS

Great men and ideas cannot function in a vacuum. There are the inescapable facts of inanimate nature—coal, steam, electricity, oil, trees, rainfall, floods. There are also the natural human necessities, such as food, shelter, and clothing. However, in emphasizing the importance of these factors, Whitehead reminds us that they are not omnipotent. "The great transitions are due to a coincidence of forces derived from *both* sides of the world, its physical and its spiritual natures."[24] In general, the influence of "geography" is explicitly recognized. He suggests that "civilization haunts the borders of waterways."[25] Referring to his own experiences, he suggests that it is not difficult to become interested in history and beauty if one is surrounded by historic remains and

[22] *R.M.,* p. 37.
[23] See A. H. Johnson, *Whitehead's Philosophy of Civilization* (Boston: Beacon Press, 1958), Chapter 3.
[24] *A.I.,* p. 21. (Italics mine.)
[25] "Harvard: The Future," p. 157 this volume.

dwells in the midst of great natural beauty. In short, "Geography is half of Character."[26]

ECONOMIC ACTIVITIES

It is the opinion of Whitehead that "the great convulsions [in human affairs] happen when the economic urge on the masses has dove-tailed with some simplified ideal end [as envisaged by the upper, directing classes]."[27] He refers to the "fusion of ideal and economic policies, making the stuff of history."[28] With this in mind, it will be obvious that when Whitehead states that "the plain economic facts of life must be the governing force in social development,"[29] he does not intend to claim that economic forces are the *only* governing forces. His point is that they must be taken into account, otherwise the ideal aims cannot be realized. Within the restrictions noted above, Whitehead gives due emphasis to the importance of economic factors in influencing the processes of human life.

The preceding discussion of (a) the meaning of civilization, (b) requisites for civilized living, and (c) decisive social factors, provides a convenient background for an examination of Whitehead's American essays in social philosophy. These essays embody and imply Whiteheadian ideas and insights concerning civilization. Adequate interpretation and appreciation of these essays requires awareness of the context, of thought and aspiration, in which they occur.

[26] "The Education of an Englishman," p. 146 this volume.
[27] *A.I.,* p. 85.
[28] *Ibid.*
[29] *Ibid.*

Interpretation of Whitehead's American Essays in Social Philosophy

<hr>

THE PROBLEM OF RECONSTRUCTION

IN 1942, the *Atlantic Monthly* published an essay by Alfred North Whitehead entitled "The Problem of Reconstruction." It is a brief statement of the basic principles which should be borne in mind while dealing with the social problems of postwar reconstruction. However, it soon becomes evident that Whitehead regards these principles as applicable to any period in human history. Indeed, his essay serves as a useful and informative general statement of topics discussed at greater length in the other essays included in this volume.

Whitehead's approach to the problems of social philosophy is indicated in the comment that "there can be no civilization apart from a well-organized system of interrelated activities."[1] However, he notes that there are many types of social order, and that groups organized in different fashions frequently engage in conflict. Hence there is need for coordination of social groups. Nevertheless, order is not the only goal of social life.

[1] p. 53. Unless otherwise indicated, all page references are to this volume.

There must be provision for novelty. The source of novelty is the creative initiative of the individual person. This must be protected if civilizaton is to survive.

In view of all this, it is wrong to claim that there is one simple unchanging formula which is applicable, in the same fashion, to all social problems at all places and all times. Such all inclusive general principles, or laws, may be useful as sources of suggestions. But their applications must either be restricted in scope or be "tailored" to meet local conditions. Rigorous addiction to traditional principles may lead to disaster. For example, it is no longer wise to advise an ambitious young man to go west in a covered wagon.

Whitehead is well aware of the fact that the goals of society depend for their realization upon many contributing factors. In a brief but enlightening historical sketch he refers to several opportunities which have arisen for the satisfaction of basic human needs. For example, with customary sanity and balanced judgment Whitehead remarks that the impressive technological developments on which the Industrial Revolution was based (e.g. the use of steam power and the resultant improvement in means of transportation) can not legitimately take all the credit for the vast changes which took place. There were also men who earlier developed basic theoretical ideas. Yet, on the other hand, too much credit can not be assigned to men and technical ideas. As Whitehead remarks with somewhat impish irony: "The thoughts of Galileo and Newton were of supreme interest, but the habits of mankind between . . . 1690 and 1750 were very slightly altered. The total effect was that fortunate people had a new theme of intellectual enjoyment. Indeed, within this period the introduction of cheap spirits, such as gin, probably did more harm to English life than all the novel thoughts of The Royal

Society did good."[2] Yet in the long run, such ideas were effective. In other words, decisive changes in human life take place slowly and are the result of the cumulative effect of many conditioning factors. No simple formula suffices.

THE STUDY OF THE PAST—ITS USES AND ITS DANGERS

In 1933, on the occasion of the twenty-fifth anniversary of the founding of The Harvard Graduate School of Business Administration, Whitehead contributed to the *Harvard Business Review* an essay entitled "The Study of the Past—Its Uses and Its Dangers."

He proceeds to show that "in our economic system as now developed there is a starvation of human impulses, a denial of opportunity, a limitation of beneficial activity—in short, a lack of freedom."[3] This point is developed at some length. It is noted that under ordinary conditions of capitalistic mass production based on technological developments, a considerable portion of the population is not gainfully employed. Many forms of employment, though unsatisfactory, are tolerated in order to sustain life and obtain a few "creature comforts." Thus the hypothetical freedom to select a satisfactory vocation is a phantasm. There is a further difficulty. The routine activities involved in mass production tend to blot out individual initiative. There is no real opportunity to cultivate the interests of the individual workman. The deadening influence of mass production on the aesthetic sensibilities of consumers is also emphasized. Here too, individual interests and tastes are either stunted or eliminated because of the necessity of selecting goods from a restricted group of "standard lines."

[2] p. 59.
[3] p. 76.

Not only are aesthetic values disregarded. Competitive business procedure (in many instances) tends to show little concern for *any* of the higher values. This neglect of the needs of individuals is ultimately self-defeating. Extensive opportunity for self-expression is the basis for progress in any field of activity.

Having sketched the chief characteristics, and noted some of the deplorable implications, of our present economic system, Whitehead offers specific suggestions concerning its improvement. (He is prepared to admit that some of his suggested reforms are now being implemented by a minority of enlightened business executives. Hence the criticisms which he has leveled at the majority do not apply to this enlightened minority.) He does not advocate the abandonment of mass production, large corporations, or private property. However, he vigorously recommends that these institutions be operated in such a fashion that they produce more adequate support for civilized living. For example, there might be an interweaving of mass production and craftsmanship. He argues that this is quite feasible in our modern world. In support of this suggestion he cites the example of France where individuality of craftsmanship and individuality of aesthetic experience have been preserved in the "finishing" of the raw material produced by mass production methods. The implementation of this suggestion would, of course, require a considerable change in attitude on the part of all concerned. For example, people will have to accept higher prices and longer production schedules. The benefits will be (a) more beautiful and substantial objects and (b) the satisfaction of a wider range of interests. If a change in attitude is to be effected, education will be the decisive agency.

In the discussion of the problem of the reform of our economic system, Whitehead states that the "business mind" must widen its range of interests, must become more clearly and systematically aware of the demands and needs which exist in human beings. In particular, an effective business man must recognize the multitude of interrelated factors that are involved in commerce. It must be realized that business is a part, but only a part, of the complex process of human existence. Business must not be conducted in isolation from consideration of the requirements of the good life for all men. Whitehead is anxious to emphasize the point that "the motive of success is not enough. It produces a short-sighted world which destroys the sources of its own prosperity."[4] He contends that we shall never have a "great society" until business men, not just saints and sages (indeed all men), are seriously concerned with all values—not just economic values but also truth, beauty, and goodness. In any case it must be realized that unregulated, completely selfish, individualistic competition produces a "resurgence of something very like industrial slavery at the base of society."[5] Modern Big Business tends to involve a feudalistic structure of organization. Such facts must be faced if economic problems are to be dealt with in a satisfactory fashion.

At the risk of apparent repetition, it seems worthwhile to call attention to Whitehead's penetrating and trenchant summary of his general position: "The curse that has been laid on humanity, in fable and in fact, is, that by the sweat of its brow shall it live. But reason and moral intuition have seen in this curse the foundation for advance. The early Benedictine monks rejoiced in their labors because they conceived themselves as thereby made fellow-workers with Christ. Stripped of its theological trappings, the essential idea remains, that work should be transfused with an in-

---

[4] *A.I.,* p. 124. (See discussion of education for business pp. 45–47, 189–193 this volume.)

[5] *A.I.,* p. 42.

tellectual and moral vision and thereby turned into a joy, triumphing over its weariness and its pain."[6]

Stated less rhetorically, Whitehead is advocating what, in part at least, efficiency experts have come to recognize. It is a fundamental fact that unless a man enjoys his work and feels that he is doing something worthwhile he will be an inefficient workman or executive. Whitehead is not interested primarily in efficiency. He is chiefly concerned with setting up conditions which make possible the development of civilization. It is important to note that "efficiency" and the "ideal" require roughly similar conditions. These changed conditions can be brought about by education, an education that will effect not only executives and laborers but also the consuming public. Men will never be able to live their lives to the full unless all men realize that the economic process must be controlled in the interest of the most worthwhile self-development of individual human beings.

If all this seems unduly optimistic, it should be noted that there are occasions when Whitehead tends to take a rather pessimistic view concerning the possibility of improving the economic status of the majority of people. "You may, perhaps, by some great reforms, obviate the worst kind of sweated labor and the insecurity of employment. But you can never greatly increase average incomes. On that side all hope of Utopia is closed to you."[7]

Whitehead sets his discussion of social problems and suggested reforms of economic evils in the context of an analysis of underlying assumptions. He shows that the emphasis on the

---

[6] A. N. Whitehead, *The Aims of Education* (New York: Macmillan, 1929), pp. 67–68. Hereafter this book will be referred to as *A.E.* (*N.B.* The page notation is the same in the Williams and Norgate, London, edition of 1932.)

[7] *A.E.*, p. 64. It should, however, be noted that this type of statement is exceptional. The general tenor of Whitehead's discussion of social problems is on the side of optimism.

ruthless competition of unregulated individuals ("pure liberalism") was strongly influenced by several dominant scientific
ideas and the philosophical position typified by Descartes. "The
doctrine of minds, as independent substances, leads directly
. . . to private worlds of morals. . . . Accordingly, self-respect,
and the making the most of your own individual opportunities,
together constituted the efficient morality of the leaders among
the industrialists of that period."[8] This helped to produce the
callous disregard of the welfare of others that was so characteristic
of some of the more fortunate members of nineteenth century
society. This point of view was further supported by the Malthusian doctrine which, "in its popular rendering, affirmed that
as a law of nature the masses of mankind could never emerge
into a high state of well-being. Still worse, biological science
drew the conclusion that the destruction of individuals was the
very means by which advance was made to higher types of
species."[9] Whitehead further calls attention to the fact that
Descartes' theory that matter is valueless justified the atrocious
disregard of natural and artistic beauty which is so characteristic
of modern society. Ugly towns and cities, defaced countrysides—
the result of blind industrial expansion—illustrate this point
with sickening clarity.

Whitehead's opposition to this general philosophy of life
(and its implications) is vehement and comprehensive. He
claims, for example, that the "philosophy of evolution" does not
justify *only* its better known implications, struggle for existence
—hence competition, class warfare, antagonism between nations—the gospel of hate. Rather, the proper conclusion to be
drawn from a careful study of evolution is fortunately of a more

[8] *S.M.W.*, p. 281.
[9] *A.I.*, p. 44.

balanced character. "Those organisms are successful which modify their environments so as to assist each other. This law is exemplified in nature on a vast scale. . . . Every organism requires an environment of friends, partly to shield it from violent changes, and partly to supply it with its wants. The Gospel of Force is incompatible with a social life."[10] Whitehead also shows, in some detail, the inadequacies of an uncritical use of the Malthusian theory. He of course admits that "struggle" is a genuine factor in the total situation. It is foolish to disregard it.

Not only is excessive emphasis on the "ruthless" implications of evolution rejected by Whitehead, he also shows that "haughty exclusiveness" is no longer a characteristic of the components of the physical or mental universes. Rather, the emphasis is on the interrelated flow of energy. "Independent substances" are museum pieces. "Exclusive individuality" has the same status.

MEMORIES and ENGLAND AND THE NARROW SEAS

Two autobiographical essays, entitled "Memories" and "England and the Narrow Seas," serve as effective media for Whitehead's discussion of some of the factors and forces which help condition the complex activities of human society.

As Whitehead aptly remarks, "the stuff of human life cannot be wholly construed in terms of historical events; [i.e., those emphasized by professional historians] it mainly consists of feelings arising from reactions between small definite groups of persons."[11] In general, "a way of life is something more than the shifting relations of bits of matter in space and in time. Life depends upon such external factors. The all-important aesthetic arises out of them, and is deflected by them. But, in abstraction

10 *S.M.W.*, pp. 296–297.
11 p. 82.

from the atmosphere of feeling, one behavior pattern is as good as another; and they are all equally uninteresting."[12]

It is obvious that Whitehead recognizes clearly the importance of great men (for example, Gladstone) in shaping the affairs of nations. However, he does not make the mistake of concentrating exclusively on one type of man. During his youth he observed the power exerted by religious leaders, men like the Archbishop of Canterbury (Tait) and by his own father, a typical clergyman of the established Church in East Kent. These men were leaders in all activities, secular as well as sacred. As members of a great institution, the Church, they brought into focus another decisive social factor.

Whitehead points out that for a time the Church was so thoroughly a part of the life of the nation that it literally was "the nation rising to the heights of civilization." Indeed the Church participated in all phases of national life. The thoroughness of the interfusion of Church and state is aptly illustrated by Whitehead. In the eleventh century the church buildings in East Kent were havens of refuge from invading pirates. The entire population of a village could find shelter behind the thick walls of the local church. From its tower, missiles could be showered on the attackers. In the days when bootlegging was a profitable business, services in the churches frequently would be suspended so that the congregation could remove the brandy stored in the church vaults to a hiding place in the marshes, safe from revenue officers. Whitehead's father, as vicar of St. Peter's Parish and canon of Canterbury Cathedral, had in his youth ridden to the hounds and played cricket with teams in the area. He gave leadership in political and educational reforms during his long career of service to his people. Indeed he was the

[12] p. 79.

guardian of the well-being of all members of the community.

In discussing great men, and the institutions which they represent, Whitehead does not lose sight of lesser men who in their own restricted fashion contribute to the life of the nation. In an effective and salutory fashion, he reminds us of the complexity of human society. He provides a wonderful portrait gallery of people whom he knew, or knew about, during his life in England. They range from prime ministers, archbishops, queens and kings, to simple rustics peddling fire wood, or rowing small boys about a safe harbor. In between (on the social scale) were silly landowners like the man who rejoiced in the doctrine of eternal damnation because it solved the problem of what would eventually happen to his neighbors. Such is the vividness of Whitehead's prose that one can almost see and hear these men. One can almost sense the presence of Old Saxby (the retired crewman of a life boat) who informed the youthful Alfred North Whitehead that "eating is a beastly habit." It was clear even to a junior mind that the old salt meant that "the great-souled way of life was to sustain it on alcoholic beverages—beer for daily life and brandy for festivals."[13]

This reference to things nautical is a reminder that Whitehead, in discussing important social factors and forces, emphasizes the facts of geography. In "England and the Narrow Seas" he provides a lucid and telling exposition of the influence of the waters between England and the continent of Europe on the destiny of men.

Whitehead, as a "Man of Kent," not to be confused with the lesser breed "Kentishmen" (who had the misfortune to live in the western part of Kent), had a deep sense of the historical riches of his native soil. The face of the land was adorned with

[13] p. 98.

monuments of the past, redolent with its supreme cultural values. In this sense also the facts of geography (i.e., the environment) are seen to exert a profound influence. The nearby church of Minster was as old as the Saxons. The Romans made their contributions to its structure. Within its walls was an oak chest left there by a Norman knight during the invasion under William the Conqueror. A few miles from the Minster Church was Canterbury Cathedral, incredibly rich in the relics of English history. No one can read Whitehead's "Memories" and "England and the Narrow Seas" without appreciating the educated Englishman's awareness of history and its sustaining power in his experience. The geographical theme reappears in his essay "The Education of an Englishman." He states, in general, that "geography is half of character," and illustrates the point by noting that the gentle climate and countryside of Dorsetshire produces kindly folk rather different from the men of obstinate and lonely thought who live in rugged Kent.

An Appeal to Sanity

The years immediately preceding World War II heard many strident voices. Obviously the world was on the brink of chaos. Most politicians and ordinary citizens were confused and powerless. Only the mad men of war seemed to have a definite purpose and effective techniques. It was in the midst of this that Alfred North Whitehead wrote "An Appeal to Sanity." In this calm and balanced analysis, he states a number of guiding principles and works out their implications with reference to the major problems of the day.

The principles which should direct the relations of nations are that (a) war provides no final and satisfactory solution; (b) each great nation has an area of responsibility; (c) there are no clear issues; (d) there are no simple solutions; (e) there are no complete solutions; (f) many of the guiding principles used by politicians are out of phase with actual events; (g) compromise must be accepted; (h) the coordination of divergent tendencies must be the goal of social life. Underlying these principles is the belief that the emotional reactions of opposing groups are of utmost importance.

On the basis of these guiding principles, Whitehead comments with incisive and comprehensive skill on the problems confronting the world in 1939. Incidentally, the problems have changed little. The principles are still impressively relevant.

The problems which Whitehead considers are (a) isolation; (b) the function of British imperialism; (c) the relations between a large aggressive nation (Germany) and a small democratic nation (Czechoslovakia); (d) the place of Russia in the world; (e) the problem of Israel; (f) the problem of the Moslem world. It is characteristic of Whitehead's organic approach to any problem that he finds it impossible to consider these questions in entirely separate analyses.

Whitehead's penetrating insight into problems on the international scale is nowhere more clearly shown than in his recognition, in 1939, of the vast extent and significance of the renaissance of the Moslem world. As he aptly remarked: "Recent discussions on international relations have been conducted by one-eyed men."[14] They have not seen the Arab and Moslem awakening. There are two hundred million Moslems in the world. We simply can not afford to overlook them. Whitehead correctly realizes that the focal point of difficulty, as far as the Moslem world is concerned, is the "holy land" called (in 1939) Palestine. Specifically, the heart of the difficulty is the presence there of

[14] p. 122.

Jews (realizing the Hebrew plans for a national home), and Arabs (with newly awakened nationalism).

Whitehead was writing before the establishment of the state of Israel, yet his general position is still extremely relevant. Illustrating his basic principles (for example, that there is no simple solution, that war solves no problems, that compromise is essential, that cooperation is the only valid technique), Whitehead puts the problem in broad historical context. After making clear the inescapable fact that the Jewish people have for centuries been responsible for creative initiative in most areas of culture, and have added much to the life of the nations in which they have lived, Whitehead calls attention to the grave dangers confronting them in Germany and in Europe in general (1939). It is obvious that they must have a national home. Indeed, he suggests that there be several "national homes," not just one in Palestine. As a matter of fact, the Arabs in the modern era have lived in Palestine as long as the Jews did in the distant past. Palestine is the focus of religious attention not only for Jews but also for Moslems and Christians. Further, the Holy Land would not have been freed in World War I without Arab assistance. Any promise made by Great Britain to Jewish leaders (The Balfour Declaration) was conditioned by reference to respect for the rights of Arab inhabitants. Any approach to the solution of the problem of Jews and Arabs in Palestine must be based on compromise and cooperation. Any attempt by Britain, or an Arab group, or a Jewish group, to impose a narrowly conceived solution will ultimately bring chaos. Whitehead notes that all three groups have unwisely made this attempt. One must not be misled by myopic dreams based on an idealized past. One must look both to the past and the future for insight, but the "look" must be calm and penetrating. Areas of the earth's surface, once unsuitable for settlement, are likely to be entirely appropriate in the future, for example parts of East Africa. Here, new Jewish national homes may well be established (as well as in Palestine).

The past is not only the foundation for future conflict (e.g., the restoration of a narrowly nationalistic "Zion"). In the Middle Ages there was a most fruitful period of cooperation between Moslem and Jew. As a result of this cooperation, much of the recorded wisdom of the ancient world was made available to modern man. For example, "Thomas Aquinas received Aristotle from it; Roger Bacon received the foundations of modern science from it."[15] In what now seems an unduly optimistic mood, Whitehead suggests that there is no reason why a future period of cooperation might not be mutually beneficial. Jewish skills could be combined with the ancient wisdom of the Moslem world, and from the Hebrew University of Jerusalem guidance for the development of the entire Near East might be provided. There are indeed intense emotional oppositions, and vast complexities, in the problem area of the Near East. Yet even if a final solution can not be reached, Whitehead sees hope of progress if a sufficiently long range view is taken.

The behavior of England in world affairs is sometimes a mystery, sometimes the subject of vehement criticism. Whitehead's discussion of the reasons why England did not feel obliged to intervene when Hitler modified the boundaries of Czechoslovakia provides at least a partial rationale. Further insight into British policy is made available by Whitehead's comments concerning the function of the British Empire and Commonwealth in the modern world.

Despite the mistakes of old fashioned British imperialism,

[15] p. 133.

Whitehead suggests that modern imperialism performs a useful and respectable service. Its chief function is guidance and co-ordination, not domination. He refers with pride to the transitions which have taken place from colony to independent nation and the continuing tendency in that direction. British troops number a few hundred thousand and are spread thinly about the world. There is not even the *appearance* of vast masses of soldiers riding rough-shod over subject populations.

Whitehead does not take an impossibly lofty moral stand with reference to war. "War can protect; it cannot create. Indeed, war adds to the brutality that frustrates creation. The protection of war should be the last resort in the slow progress of mankind towards its far-off ideals."[16]

The Importance of Friendly Relations Between England and the United States

The attempt to interpret the British approach to international problems which constituted one of the main themes of "An Appeal to Sanity," is continued in a speech made at Phillips Academy and reprinted in the *Phillips Bulletin*. The successful development from colony to nation (Dominion) by British possessions is sketched in greater detail. In short, Whitehead is arguing that England, like the United States, is at heart a non-military and fraternal nation. Indeed he contends that "the United States of today, and the England of today, are parallel, though diverse, developments of one great tradition of civilized life."[17]

It may be objected that the first part of this address is some-

[16] p. 135.
[17] p. 137. (It should be noted that the terms "England" and "Britain" are used as synonyms, although this is a convenience which may not appeal to some readers.)

what optimistic in its references to England and America. The common ideals are stressed, similarities are emphasized. Facts in refutation undoubtedly will occur to a person versed in history. Whitehead would reply that he is referring to England and America of today. Doubts may still remain. Further, recent events reveal the excessive optimism of Whitehead's claim that only in the remote future could America's safety be threatened by China or Russia. In any case, the latter part of the speech strikes, at least for a time, a somber note. He has no doubt that it is America's destiny to be supreme in the world. Whitehead warns his audience of the terrible mistakes which may be made by Americans as they assume world leadership. In serious tones he remarks that "history has no mercy upon those who, having the opportunity [for world leadership], allow themselves to be thrust aside."[18] With deep feeling, he states that "in my own life-time, I have seen England commit errors—indeed crimes—for which there is no defence."[19] The implication is clear—there is the possibility that America may do the same. Yet there is a balancing ground for hope. Whitehead continues to say "I have seen it [England] rise to standards of conduct whose glory, as I believe, will stand for ever."

One of the grave dangers confronting any nation is the failure to recognize the passage of time and resultant changes. As Whitehead expresses it in pungent phraseology, "it is criminal not to know in time when some old maxim of prudent statescraft does not apply to the case immediately before you."[20] For example (the illustration is implicit though not stated by Whitehead), the day has come when it is no longer sane to regard

[18] pp. 141–142.
[19] p. 142.
[20] p. 142.

native Africans as gentle children of the forest who can be satisfied by the presentation of beads and cast-off clothing. There must be friendly sympathy and comprehending assistance in the process of self-development. These attitudes are essential in our dealings with nations at all stages of civilization. This is no lofty abstract moral code. As Whitehead points out, it is based on self-interest. The simple fact of the matter is that "we cannot do without each other."[21] The boys to whom Whitehead spoke are now the leaders of an America which has found it difficult to implement this advice.

THE EDUCATION OF AN ENGLISHMAN

Whitehead's essay "The Education of an Englishman," as has been noted, continues several of the themes which are dominant in "Memories" and "England and the Narrow Seas." Here he continues his impressive treatment of the impact of "geography" on character, the influence of the historic past ever present in the form of historic sites and buildings. There are additional word portraits of types of English personality. However, the main purpose of this essay is to reveal the nature of classical education in a good English school during the latter part of the last century.

As Whitehead aptly remarks, "we think in generalities, but we live in detail."[22] The principles of a classical education are effectively illustrated in the details of Whitehead's life at Sherborne School.

He makes it clear that the Greeks impressed English classical schoolmasters and students far more than did the Romans. Roman life became debauched. The Latin language presented serious deterrents to accurate expression. Whitehead also remarks

[21] p. 142.
[22] p. 144.

elsewhere (in *The Aims of Education,* Chapter 5) that the literature of Rome is much inferior to that of Greece—inferior even to English literature. In discussing classical literature, Whitehead makes some interesting comments on the problem of translation. Unlike many classical scholars he regards "the classics in translation" as respectable. Such an approach, under proper auspices, provides a breadth of insight and appreciation which is a necessary foundation for the labors involved in translation undertaken by a beginning student.

Returning to the previous theme, an evaluation of Rome, Whitehead points out that the Romans were insufferably arrogant. On the other hand, the Greeks preached the golden mean. This was an ideal which Englishmen needed. As Whitehead remarks, it served a very useful and necessary function "sometimes moderating our national arrogance."[23] Also, sometimes it reinforced "our natural stupidity." Englishmen appreciated the Greeks fully and felt deep bonds of sympathy. The Greeks were "our kind of people," in the opinion of most Englishmen. The Greek navy, like the British navy, sailed narrow seas (the Mediterranean). Both nations looked to the east. Alexander in his eastern conquests was like Clive in India. Yet, even in the midst of his praises of "things Greek," Whitehead does not lose sight of Rome's "sense of greatness."

Greek (like Latin) was not regarded as a foreign language. It was a normal tool. For example, the Bible was read in Greek. Only the very young descended to the vulgarity of reading it in English. The concentration on Greek classics was supplemented by some mathematics, science, French, and a few plays of Shakespeare. Only the first of these subjects was presented effectively. As Whitehead reports, this curriculum was "a curious mixture

[23] p. 152.

of imaginative appeal and precise, detailed knowledge."[24] Discipline outside the classroom was handled by the head boy (prefect). Whitehead recalls functioning in this capacity and whipping a boy in front of his assembled classmates for stealing. Games were organized and controlled by the boys themselves. Masters participated only on invitation.

Such a school did not deliberately prepare men for a life in industry. It was not concerned with this aspect of the modern world. It was designed to train men to "serve God in Church and State." It did produce eminent bishops and military commanders. Whitehead admits that it was "a deplorably narrow education to fit us for the modern world."[25] Yet he stands firm in his conviction that it produced graduates richer in political imagination than the graduates of the Harvard School of Politics and Government.

Whitehead's discussion of classical education in its flower is a valuable point of reference for those who find it difficult to appreciate this approach to education, or for those who wish to return to the "good old" days of classical education. Further, an examination of Whitehead's youthful educational experiences serves as an excellent background for the appreciation of his magnificent essay on modern university education, "Harvard: The Future," and also the less comprehensive essays dealing with the same topic, "Historical Changes" and "Universities and Their Function."

HARVARD: THE FUTURE, HISTORICAL CHANGES, and UNIVERSITIES AND THEIR FUNCTION

The celebration in 1936 of the three-hundredth anniversary of the founding of Harvard College naturally stimulated a great

[24] p. 153.
[25] p. 155.

deal of serious thought concerning the future of Harvard in particular and American universities in general. Few men were better fitted than Alfred North Whitehead to engage in a process of evaluation and suggestion.

His justly famous essay "Harvard: The Future" is an impressive example of his efficacy in the field of philosophy of education. In earlier writings he had formulated basic educational principles and applied them chiefly to problems in primary and secondary education. In "Harvard: The Future," he focuses attention on these principles as they apply to education in its fullest stage of development, at the university level. It is to be noted that Whitehead tends to use the term "Harvard" in a generic sense to refer to all universities of this type.

Whitehead is convinced that the fate of civilization no longer depends on the efforts of churches. Rather, it rests in the hands of the great universities. In a few incisive sentences he sets the problem: "Once Babylon had its chance and produced the Tower of Babel. The University of Paris fashioned the intellect of the Middle Ages. Will Harvard fashion the intellect of the twentieth century?"[26] And if so, in what fashion? The principles which must guide a university, if it is to fulfill its destiny and serve society adequately, were recognized, at least in part, long ago by Plato. Stated briefly and in general terms they are (a) Learning should be a self-activated process of acquisition, not passive receptivity. (b) Experience is vast and complex. Both vagueness and clarity characterize it. New insights are constantly being obtained. Hence there is no room for dogmatic claims of absolute certainty. (c) Knowledge should be used in an attempt to control the flux of experience.

Whitehead's position is the exact antithesis of the widely held

[26] p. 158.

view that it is the business of the university to dispense lofty, abstract, exact, clear knowledge—and keep out of practical affairs.

Specifically, he criticizes the customary distinction between certain, clear, exact knowledge (as in mathematics) and probable, unclear, inexact opinion (as in hasty sensory observation). It is a useful distinction but can not be made uncritically. As a matter of fact, even in mathematics there is no agreement concerning what is clear and certain. Whitehead reports that every generalization in mathematical physics, which he was taught as a student at Cambridge in the years 1880–1885, has since been modified or abandoned. With customary ironic humor he remarks that the "history of thought is largely concerned with the records of clear-headed men insisting that they at last have discovered some clear, adequately expressed, indubitable truths. If clear-headed men throughout the ages would only agree with each other, we might cease to be puzzled."[27]

The fact that we do not have the certainty, clarity, and exactness which some men claim does not justify a relapse into craven skepticism and the abandonment of all effort to extend and apply knowledge.

Whitehead's main point seems to be that much factual knowledge has been obtained which, for practical purposes, need not be doubted. However, we should not nourish illusions about absolute certainty, clarity, and exactness. Other information should be regarded as even less reliable than the usually accepted information. Yet even these apparent distinctions in status of information should be open to profound suspicion. Our experience is a complex mixture of vagueness and clarity in varying degrees. Every item of experience is interrelated with numerous

[27] pp. 160–161.

other items. A complete, comprehensive, clear, and exact grasp of the organic whole of things is simply beyond us. As Whitehead once remarked, "We should seek clarity and distrust it."

One of the greatest calamities which has come to reduce the efficacy of universities (and it is a continuing threat) is the worship of the dictionary—the belief that knowledge can be fully expressed in clearly defined words or mathematical symbols. This is the fallacy of the perfect dictionary. No such book can be found in the library of any university. As a matter of fact, the rich complexity of life can not be compressed within the limits of available language. There are emotions, thoughts, and actions which simply escape the grasp of verbal or other symbols. For example the young man in love, or the athlete in the excitement of victory, is somewhat inarticulate. Even the well trained scientist seems unable to convey all aspects of his discoveries to his colleagues.

The addiction to clearly defined words and simple ideas not only leads us away from the vague complexities of experience which are sometimes of basic importance; worse still, the devotees of simplicity and clarity tend to fracture the universe into artificially separate and distinct items. They then concentrate attention on a few of them. Thus a strange myopia develops. For example, a scientist may view a man as merely matter in motion, and neglect moral, aesthetic, and spiritual aspects. A moralist, on the other hand, may be so concerned with a lofty moral ideal, clearly and simply stated, that he forgets the surges of passion and complex environmental pressures which beset human existence. The good life, the civilized life, must not neglect any phase of experience. Also, we must go behind the words to the facts and values to which they refer. Knowledge in the true sense is based on "revelation," direct insight, that is, immediate experience.

Information should be forward looking and "suffused with suggestiveness." For "human nature loses its most precious quality when it is robbed of its sense of things beyond, unexplored and yet insistent."[28] As Whitehead says in "Universities and Their Function," the main purpose of a university is not to convey factual information and confront students with the possibility of value experience, important as these functions are. Other institutions (e.g., research laboratories of industry, libraries, churches) can do that. The main function is to acquaint the students with facts and values illuminated by, and clothed in, imagination. Under these conditions facts are no longer weights on the memory. They are data useful in solving real problems. Values are no longer impossible ideals. Imagination shows how they may be translated into action. Thus an imaginative approach to life is not an escape. It is the supreme basis of efficacy. It follows that a university professor should wear his learning imaginatively and not act as a final authority dictating absolute truth for inclusion in the student's note book. Rather, the professor should appear as a relatively ignorant man, using his small store of information to solve what problems he can, probing always into the mysteries beyond the relative certainties of the present frontiers of information.

In his incisive address to Harvard business students entitled "Foresight" (which appeared as a preface to Dean W. B. Donham's book, *Business Adrift*), Whitehead stresses an educational principle which is particularly important. He refers to "the vicious assumption that each generation will substantially live

[28] p. 166.

amid the conditions governing the lives of its fathers and will transmit those conditions to mould with equal force the lives of its children."[29] This assumption is vicious, indeed deadly, because of the present very rapid acceleration in the rate of social change, indeed of change in all areas of human experience. It is impossible, in this day, to equip a person with a set of technical skills, political, educational, social, religious, and other doctrines which will remain effective to "see him through" to the end of his life. Today's mechanical skill may tomorrow be a "drug on the market." Time-honored political beliefs now go out of date in a few years—for example, the belief that America can afford isolation because of the protection of surrounding oceans. In all honesty and fairness then, we must train our young people, and this is particularly true of university education, to expect novelty. There can be no detailed preparation for the unknown future. The best that one can expect is the development of powers of imaginative foresight. A person who studies the past and present with care has at least the hope of anticipating some of the future, relatively novel, developments which will take place. But, to repeat, imagination is essential.

Whitehead's views concerning the place, and relative importance, of novelty in the life of man are effectively clarified in his essay entitled "Historical Changes." This appeared in *The Radcliffe Quarterly.* It served as his tribute on the occasion of the fiftieth anniversary of the founding of Radcliffe College. The establishment of Radcliffe was a striking novelty. Its fiftieth anniversary called attention to the vast change which had taken place in the status of women in American society.

With characteristic philosophic insight Whitehead attempts to place the general fact of novelty in proper perspective. It is

[29] *A.I.*, p. 117.

not new or localized. One of the first philosophers, Heraclitus, called attention to its existence by his famous remark that one can not cross (or even step into) the same river twice.

But our appreciation of the value of creative change must be balanced by an appreciation of the value of the past as a vital ingredient in our lives. As Whitehead aptly remarks, "what our students should learn is how to face the future with the aid of the past."[30] This appreciation and use of the past does not involve slavish and uncritical imitation. The ancestral voices are sometimes irrelevant and sometimes don't know what they are talking about. Yet, proper appreciation of the past may save us from unfortunate uncritical use of apparently novel ideas. As Whitehead once remarked, he who pays no attention to the wisdom of the past is doomed to repeat the mistakes of his grandfathers.

Whitehead concludes his remarks to the joyful and proud ladies of Radcliffe by pointing out that they stand in the tradition of early pioneer women who from the past provide the basis of greatness for future generations. The present generation must revitalize the indomitable spirit of these pioneers, and like them strive "to enlarge the boundaries of life."

Whitehead contends that any educational experience should involve three distinguishable, though interfused, phases. Elsewhere, he terms them (in *The Aims of Education,* Chapter 2) the stages of *romance, precision,* and *generalization.* In the beginning there must be genuine interest, enthusiasm, enjoyment. The problem or topic must be real and vital to the student. Next comes the stage of precision, the disciplined study of relevant material and the acquiring of skills. The only effective form of discipline is self-discipline. It is made tolerable and significant

[30] p. 180.

by the preceding and continuing enthusiasm of the stage of romance. Finally, there is the stage of generalization when, having obtained insight concerning basic laws and principles, and profiting from the discipline which issues in competence (e.g., the acquisition of the necessary facts and skills), a person once again is chiefly aware of enjoyment and vital interest. In this fashion Whitehead thinks the dual claims of (a) novelty of enjoyment and freedom in the satisfaction of basic human needs and (b) the inescapable requirements of order and discipline can be met.

Primary school is chiefly the period in which the world should appear as an interesting challenge. During these years the child should plunge eagerly into an enjoyable examination of the immediate environment. During secondary school he must, for the most part, settle down to acquire facts and skills. It is hard work. There is no royal road to learning. Yet the glow of early enthusiasm should remain as a dynamic and soothing factor. At the university a person should, Whitehead suggests, predominantly enjoy the increased efficiency and scope which is based on the hard work of the secondary school period. He should turn from arduous and major concentration on particular facts and problems. Then he should master general laws and principles which can be applied to relevant problems in his daily life. The successful university graduate, Whitehead suggests with somewhat rhetorical and exaggerated humor, must be prepared to burn his lecture notes, lose his text books, and forget the minutiae crammed for examination. This can and should be done if he has acquired the generality of outlook and habits of mind which render him sufficiently flexible to deal with a set of problems concerning which he has attained professional competence. In a similar fashion he should deal with other problems in fields where he has high "amateur" standing.

Thus, in summary, Whitehead remarks that education should be seen "under the aspect of a guide in the adventures of life."[31] More specifically, "applications are part of . . . knowledge." It is wrong to argue that one must first acquire knowledge and then, perhaps later, put it to use. There must be a continuous intermingling of theory and practice. This is one of the best ways to ensure that knowledge will be suffused with "suggestiveness." (The other way is the play of "vagrant thought" in the realm of abstract ideas.) Therefore Whitehead is a stern opponent of the policy of setting up a university in an "ivory tower" far removed from the pressure of ordinary events. "Celibacy does not suit a university. It must mate itself with action."[32]

Thus a true university need not always offer apologies for the existence of its professional schools of law, medicine, theology, education, and business. As a matter of fact, the tendency to segregate universities from the "real world" of practical affairs is a recent development. The great medieval universities did not make that mistake, nor did the Greeks. Plato concerned himself with complex political experiments. Aquinas taught and also participated in ecclesiastical and secular problems. In the modern world, John Locke at Oxford helped to shape the political and educational life of England.

Because of his deep personal interest in the Harvard Graduate School of Business Administration, Whitehead illustrates, in "Universities and their Function," some of his main educational themes by reference to business education. He is concerned to show the great value of theory to a man whose interests are mainly practical. If a person is to achieve maximum efficiency in business, he must have a broad background of theoretical knowl-

[31] p. 169. See also "Universities and their Function."
[32] p. 170.

edge. In addition to the obvious value of economics there is the need to understand political, sociological, psychological, religious, and cultural laws and principles. If he has a position with a large corporation with world wide contacts, geography will be of importance. At a university the future business man should acquire the ability to clothe his theoretical knowledge with imaginative insight so that he will be able to understand the thoughts and feelings of other men. Unless he is able to do this, he will not deal effectively with producers, consumers, competitors, and members of the general public. Further, his comprehensive view of the nature of a business organization will enable him to see himself in proper perspective, and help him to tolerate the initial years of his business life when perhaps his upward progress is not exactly meteoric. That is to say, he will understand why he must first go slowly in "learning the ropes."

Yet in the midst of this program of acquiring business efficiency, the student must not be allowed to lose sight of much more comprehensive and important goals. A business school should function in an environment in which young men may develop those qualities of civilized living which characterize the ideal business man described by Whitehead (in his discussion of necessary economic reforms). In short, business efficiency should be regarded as merely an instrument to be used in facilitating the fine art of adventure in the realms of truth, beauty, goodness, and peace.

The practical questions arises: How is it possible to ensure that university life will provide for a fruitful interfusion of theory and practice? Above all, how is it possible to ensure that facts, skills, laws, and principles will be vitalized by imaginative appreciation? Whitehead, of course, admits that there is no simple and easy solution. But, at least by implication, he contends that the key factor in the situation is the faculty. "Collect an able, vigorous faculty and give it a free hand."[33] As a former dean, he is well aware of the difficulties involved.

It is Whitehead's solemn conviction that the universities like Harvard have an opportunity analogous "to that of Greece after Marathon, to that of Christian institutions amid the decay of civilization."[34] Both greatly enriched human life. There was, as well, tragic failure. The future of the twentieth century is not predetermined. If its way of life is to be characterized by adventure and the achievement of peace, appreciation of art and devotion to truth, beauty, and goodness, this will come about chiefly because its universities have risen to the occasion.

SUMMARY

The preceding interpretative exposition of Whitehead's theory of civilization and of the main ideas expressed in his American essays in social philosophy has incorporated suggested evaluations. The evaluations have dealt with Whitehead's general principles and with practical applications. For the most part these comments have been favorable. It has been noted that Whitehead's approach is marked by a sane, balanced comprehensiveness which is often lacking in other treatments of these topics. In matters of detail, he is frequently impressive in his suggested solutions for specific problems. Despite his emphasis on lofty ideas he, like Dewey, is well aware of the linkage between means and ends. His is an idealism based on an enlightened realistic recognition of the hard and restraining facts of the existing environment.

It is possible to point to some instances where he is lacking

[33] p. 168.
[34] p. 176.

in accuracy when referring to possible future events. For example, he did not foresee the rapid rise of Russia and China to positions of great power. He did not appreciate the imminence of their threat to American security. He strikes some critics as relatively naive in his reliance on education as a means for reforming hard-bitten business men and as an agency for persuading the general public to accept a fusion of mass production and a reinstated craftsmanship. Despite his emphasis on emotional factors he seems unduly optimistic concerning the possibilities of rational persuasion. Yet he offers factual evidence to support this optimism, for example, the industry of France, and the relations of Great Britain to former colonies. One may legitimately protest that while Whitehead is well aware of the threat to civilization posed by piratical business men, he is not equally aware of the destructive tendencies of some labor leaders and their unions.

A carping critic may protest that these so-called "American essays" devote excessive attention to events in England. In reply it may be remarked that Whitehead performs a great service to the cause of American-British cooperation by pointing out the common elements in the experiences of the two nations. Further, he has assisted greatly in making England's "imperial" policies more understandable to the American mind. Finally, his references to England (and other countries) indicate that his general principles do not have a merely local application to American life.

It is customary, in some circles, to accuse Whitehead of being trite, obvious, a peddler of platitudes. It is true that he states ideas which have occurred to other men, have been expressed by other men. Some of these ideas are widely accepted, at least in the sense that they are given lip service. Yet, as Whitehead himself remarked, there is a real need that these obvious ideals be kept constantly before this generation, as long as they suffer from respect which does not issue in action. In any case, few men have Whitehead's skill in stating the accepted and obvious in striking, challenging form. Some of Whitehead's insights soar far beyond the mere platitudinous. To those who glory in the complexities of metaphysics or, on the other hand, seek solace in the thin realm of grammatical or logical proficiency, Whitehead's non-technical discussion of social philosophy is abhorrent. But Whitehead is second to no man in metaphysical skill and facility in manipulating the symbols of abstract thought. He has a deep concern for ordinary language. He makes better use of it than most men who pride themselves on their performances in this medium. Whitehead, in some phases of his work, wishes to speak to the average citizen. In these essays he has done so with impressive artistry. This phase of his philosophy is, of course, only one strand in his complex intellectual achievement. This literary, humanistic tendency is interwoven with a more technical approach to the problems of human existence. The technical and the non-technical ultimately provide mutual support, one for the other. They can, however, be examined in relative differentiation. This is necessary in order to experience the full flavor of each. The highest form of aesthetic achievement, as Whitehead aptly remarks, involves a unity of distinguishable diversities.

Whitehead's American essays in social philosophy are an effective and essential ingredient in his total and comprehensive discussion of man and his place in nature. They bear witness to the keenness of his insight, the depth and balanced sanity of his purpose as a philosopher. They are an impressive contribution to the literature of our western civilization.

PART TWO   THE AMERICAN ESSAYS

   Whitehead's ten American essays in social philosophy are here reprinted in their original form, although not in chronological sequence. They have been rearranged to present first Whitehead's statement of general social principles. This is followed by those essays in which he discusses problems of internal social reform and the factors which influence human societies. Next come those essays in which Whitehead is primarily concerned with international relations. Last are the essays dealing specifically with educational problems.

STATEMENT OF GENERAL PRINCIPLES
   The Problem of Reconstruction (*Atlantic Monthly*, Vol. 169, 1942)

SOCIAL REFORM AND FACTORS WHICH INFLUENCE
HUMAN SOCIETIES
   The Study of the Past—Its Uses and Its Dangers (*Harvard Business Review*, Vol. 11, 1933)
   Memories (*Atlantic Monthly*, Vol. 157, 1936)
   England and the Narrow Seas (*Atlantic Monthly*, Vol. 139, 1927)

INTERNATIONAL RELATIONS
   An Appeal to Sanity (*Atlantic Monthly*, Vol. 163, 1939)
   The Importance of Friendly Relations Between England and the United States (*Phillips Bulletin*, Vol. XIX, 1925)

EDUCATION
   The Education of an Englishman (*Atlantic Monthly*, Vol. 138, 1926)
   Harvard: The Future (*Atlantic Monthly*, Vol. 158, 1936)
   Historical Changes (*Radcliffe Quarterly*, Vol. 14, 1930)
   Universities and Their Function (*Atlantic Monthly*, Vol. 141, 1928)

I

The Problem of Reconstruction

I

I SHOULD like to discuss the special problem of political reconstruction after the war. The reader will understand that I am concerned only with the general outlook.

We shall be faced with a completely disrupted social system, in confusion physically, emotionally, and ideologically. This statement certainly applies to Europe, and to large portions of Asia and Africa. Also it must be remembered that sociological disruption is the most contagious disease known to mankind. Thus the first requisite is that order be imposed. There can be no civilization apart from a well-organized system of interrelated activities, within which the intimacies of family life can be developed.

Human life discloses many types of social order existing in the world, and—what is more perplexing—a great antagonism between adjacent groups in respect to differences of kinds of order, kinds of emotion, and individual human beings produced by those various types. The love of humanity as such is mitigated by violent dislike of the next-door neighbor.

For this reason, no single world-wide solution of the social problem can be successfully adopted. Each special district must be studied with a view to the immediate solution applicable to it. There can be no one general system of social coordination which does not destroy the special capacities of smaller groups. The essence of the world-wide sociological problem is the study of the modes of grouping mankind subject to some coordination of the various groups. Of course, this conclusion is a commonplace for all successful government. In this country there are forty-eight states, and the District of Columbia, all supervised by the central government. Also in each state there are cities, and townships, and counties, each with its freedom of action within limits.

Thus there must be a careful study of the possibilities of grouping, and of coordinating groups in different areas—for example, in the Mahometan world of the Middle East, including Egypt; and in Central Europe, stretching from the Baltic to the Aegean Sea, with Russia and the Mahometan world on one side and Germany and Italy on the other. Then there is Western Europe, with its various groupings. Also there is the coordination of these groups.

But we have omitted the fact that, owing to modern techniques, the world in the future will be immeasurably more compact than in past history. India, and China, and the Oceanic Islands of the Eastern and Southern Oceans, and the two Americas which separate the ancient East from the ancient West, will be in essential, immediate connection with the small European and Mahometan worlds which first claimed attention. Traditional statesmanship must be infused with the dramatic novelty which the immediate future presents. The people most responsible for this duty can compare the modes of action in the past with the novel possibilities of the future. It is their business to inform the populations and to guide the statesmen. Above all, it is their business to cooperate with each other, and not to exaggerate the petty views of the universe which their own specialties present.

II

A stable order is necessary, but it is not enough. There must be satisfaction for the purposes that are inherent in human life. Undoubtedly the first essential requirement is the satisfaction of the necessities of bodily life—food, clothing, shelter. These economic factors are dominant up to the level of moderate enjoyment. They then almost suddenly become the mere background for those experiences which form the distinction between mankind and the animal world. It is the imaginative originality of mankind that produces ideals, good or bad. We live guided by a variety of impulses—towards loving relationship, towards friendship, towards other types of enjoyment such as games, art, ideals of mutual enterprise, and ideals disclosing some sense of immortality. This intimate development of human experience enters into political theory as respect for each individual life. It demands a social structure supplying freedom and opportunity for the realization of objectives beyond the simple bodily cravings.

Of course any one group of human beings, however large, has a very finite set of appetitions, depending on past history and on the sort of prevalent ideals. In every social system there are exceptions, mostly foolish, but some of them beyond price. It is of the essence of good government to provide some adequacy of satisfaction both for the large communal motives and for all reasonable exceptions on which progress depends. It cannot be repeated too often that the only security for progress is a sincere respect for each individual human being.

As we approach these problems the first words that occur to us are "freedom" and "democracy." "Freedom" apart from relevant "opportunity" is a meaningless notion. Robinson Crusoe could do what he liked on his island: but, until the savages turned up, there was nothing for him to do. The history of mankind with its wars is the tale of groups of people seeking opportunity by the oppression of their neighbors. Sometimes these wars sink into minor disturbances and are conventionalized, as in the late Middle Ages and in the eighteenth century.

The enthusiasm for crusades—Mahometans attacking Christians or Christians attacking Mahometans—illustrates the poverty of life in the Middle Ages. Also slavery, or half-slavery, by eliminating the claims of a large portion of the population, preserved the limited store of opportunity for the fortunate minority. Today the notion of a master race is being revived, and most of us are agreed that it means the moral degradation of mankind.

Within the last four centuries there have been three dramatic disclosures of new large-scale opportunities. I put aside the Italian Renaissance, for it concerned only a fortunate minority. It was the last spurt of the Middle Ages. Thomas Aquinas would have enjoyed it.

The first disclosure was the discovery of a new world—namely, the half-empty continent of America, as the immediate result of the new technique of oceanic voyaging. The real discovery was in fact the new art of navigation, and America was the first gift derived from it. The history of civilization opens a new chapter at this period, by reason of this increase of opportunity. The problem of existence was not solved; but hope entered into human life as never before. The three countries most concerned—

namely, Spain, the Netherlands, and England—for the period of about one hundred and fifty years, starting with the sixteenth century, exhibited a stage of excited hopefulness, while unfortunate Germany was torn to pieces by disputes inherited from the mediaeval world. France was balanced between the two periods, and developed the brilliance of the old European civilization. The intensity of the French Revolution showed that novel opportunity had not penetrated throughout the nation.

The second enlargement of opportunity began about two and a half centuries after the first. It was the Industrial Revolution, which gradually developed from the middle of the eighteenth century, with its two culminations in the invention of the steam engine and the invention of the railway. Human life was transformed.

I am inclined to believe that its best effect was in opening the whole extent of North America to the European population. This was due to the steamboat and the railway. But nothing great in human history is due to a single cause; and we must also add the influence during the American Revolution of great statesmen guiding a peculiarly intelligent people.

At least the new techniques transformed life throughout the world, more especially in Europe and America. In Western Europe during the second quarter of the nineteenth century there was a period of optimism. The problem of human life seemed to have been solved, and the first International Exhibition in London, during the year 1851, celebrated this glorious triumph with the creation of the famous Crystal Palace.

Alas, something was missing. It may have been the want of intelligence among statesmen and industrial leaders. It may have been that the development of techniques was less fundamental than it seemed. Whatever the reason, the Crystal Palace, very symbolically, has been burnt down; and the nations are now struggling to avoid the ancient evil, which is the selfish mastery of the few over the many.

At the present time we are in the first phase of the third enlargement of opportunity, perhaps the most important crisis in the history of civilization.

The intellectual development of mankind, with its self-conscious criticism has a recent growth of some five or six thousand years. Its earlier stages seem to consist of traditional legend with the minimum of coordination. But about two thousand and six hundred years ago a widespread movement of critical judgment on the nature of things had established itself. The European races derive their special systems of thought from the brilliant races in the Eastern Mediterranean and the Near East, more especially from the Greeks. But in the course of ages the centre of activity has moved backwards and forwards through many races from Mesopotamia to the Strait of Gibraltar. It has also spread northward. There were analogous movements in China and India; and the three intellectual growths fed each other intermittently. But the European systematic thought has shown the greatest energy both in self-criticism and by its contact with practical activity. Today it is refashioning the ways of thought and action in every civilized race of the world.

The result has been a gradual broadening of opportunity. But this growth has been intermittent and wavering. Slavery became serfdom, and serfdom became free laborers on the edge of starvation. The status of the workers improved, although the slums of industrial cities disgraced industry. Indeed, at the very moment when the Industrial Revolution was in its prime Malthus managed to prove that the mass of mankind must always live on the verge of starvation. He was answered only by the nearest approach to an appeal to Divine Providence that men like John Stuart Mill dared to make. Every factor involved in human existence is too variable to justify these sweeping statistical deductions based on past experience.

As an historic fact, the gradual introduction of novel techniques has broadened the amplitude of opportunity for the mass of mankind, slowly and waveringly. Within the past five or six hundred years there have been certain crises in this slow advance, due to these novel techniques. These critical techniques are not the most interesting facts for abstract thinkers, but their immediate effect was overwhelming. For example, the evolution of transoceanic navigation, as distinct from coastal voyaging, is not very interesting for abstract learning. But it changed the history of mankind. Again, the thoughts of Galileo and Newton were of supreme interest, but the habits of mankind between the dates 1690 and 1750 were very slightly altered. The total effect was that fortunate people had a new theme of intellectual enjoyment. Indeed, within this period the introduction of cheap spirits, such as gin, probably did more harm to English life than all the novel thoughts of the Royal Society did good. But the growth of science did arouse an alertness of intellect. The result was the Industrial Revolution in the hundred years between 1750 and 1850.

III

Today we are at the beginning of a new crisis of civilization, which gives promise of producing more fundamental change than any preceding advance. The growth of science in every department of thought seems to have reached a stage where the whole spread of knowledge discloses new possibilities for practice. This holds throughout the whole range of activities, from medicine to engineering, from mining to aerial flight, from the use of the microscope to the waves of energy from remote nebulae, from psychoanalysis to geology. The whole of human practical activity is in process of immediate transformation by novelties of organized knowledge. It is no longer a question of a new detail such as gunpowder, or printing, or the power of steam or novel machinery, or a new aspect of religious thought. Today the whole extent of learned thought is transforming every activity of mankind. This is the largest epoch in human history. Historical knowledge is essential, but very dangerous. The old phrases are misleading. For example, in this country it is no longer sufficient to tell young people to "go West in a covered wagon." In my own country, the old habits must be completely reformed. Again, we must insist, history is essential for the direction of action, but its naive application is very dangerous.

Still more dangerous are the simple-minded generalizations of specialized scientists beyond their own limits of special knowledge. The truth is that we must work together. Historians must study the new possibilities of action; and scientists must learn the old checkered history of human emotion passing into large-scale social activities.

There is one prophecy upon which I will venture. It is that throughout the vast land areas of the Old World—Russia and China, for instance—the example of North America will be predominant. Perhaps also America has something to learn from Russia and China.

Also, forgive me when I conclude with a confession of personal political faith. I do not trust any extreme, abstract plan of universal social construction. Such plans are important for the stimulation of the imagination. But in practice every successful advance is a compromise. The general ideal is the wide diffusion of opportunity. The sort of opportunity relevant to each special case depends on special characteristics of the populations involved.

II

The Study of the Past—Its Uses
and Its Dangers

For each succeeding generation, the problem of Education is new. What at the beginning was enterprise, after the lapse of five and twenty years has become repetition. All the proportions belonging to a complex scheme of influences upon our students have shifted in their effectiveness. In the lecture halls of a university, as indeed in every sphere of life, the best homage which we can pay to our predecessors to whom we owe the greatness of our inheritance is to emulate their courage.

In allusion to the title of this address—"The Study of the Past, Its Uses and Its Dangers"—I may at once say that the main danger is the lack of discrimination between the details which are now irrelevant and the main principles which urge forward human existence, ever renewing their vitality by incarnation in novel detail.

THE PRESENT A TURNING POINT IN
WESTERN CIVILIZATION

It so happens that the first five and twenty years of the existence of the Harvard Graduate School of Business Administration exactly coincides with a turning point in the sociological conceptions of Western Civilization. Here, by the term Western Civilization, I mean the sociological habits of the European races from the Ural Mountains on the boundary of Asia passing westward half way round the world to the shores of the Pacific Ocean, that is from 60° east longitude to rather more than 120° west longitude.

If you keep to the northern temperate zone, in every country that you can pass through in this long journey you will find some profound agitation, examining and remodeling the ways of social life handed down from the preceding four hundred years. This agitation as a major feature in social life is the product of the past twenty-five years. Of course this unrest has its long antecedents, but within this final short period the disturbance has become dominant. Undoubtedly, something has come to an end.

It is also worth noticing that the center of disturbance seems to lie within each country. We are not dealing with the repercussions of a revolution with one local center. In Russia there has been a revolution, because something has come to an end. In Asia Minor the Turks are recreating novel forms of social life, because something has come to an end. Throughout Central Europe, every nation is in a ferment, because something has come to an end. With one exception in the larger nations of Western Europe, Italy, Spain, Germany, England, there is a turmoil of reconstruction, because something has come to an end. The one exception is France. In that country, the internal motive seems to be absent—perhaps fortunately for her. But anyhow, the comparative absence of any feeling of the end of ways of procedure explains a certain inability to penetrate instinctively into the springs of action of her neighboring nations. For the rest of Europe, something has come to an end; while France is

prepared to resume the practice of traditions derived from Riche-
lieu, from Turgot, from the French Revolution, and above all
from her incomparable craftsmen.

When in this survey we cross the Atlantic and come to America, I do not think that there is exaggeration in the refrain, that
something has come to an end. We stand at the commencement
of a new thrust in sociological functioning, and this novelty is of
supreme importance in respect to the education of our future
leaders in business administration. Do not misunderstand me.
In each nation we all want to continue the aim at our old ideals.
We can only preserve the essence of the past by the embodiment
of it in novelty of detail. I will anticipate the argument by stating my belief that the best feature in the past was the sturdy individualism fostered by the conditions of those times. I am here
referring to the last two centuries in the life of America, of
England, and of Continental Europe. Why I have drawn attention to the universality of the present sickness is to draw the
conclusion that the remedy is not to be found in the adjustment
of some detail peculiar to any one nation. In each nation there
will be details of change peculiar to it, and between nations
there will be differences of proportion. But we are not likely to
recognize the necessary group of details unless we have some
grasp of the general character of the disease.

The Preceding Trend from Mediaevalism
to Individualism

What has come to an end is a mode of sociological functioning
which from the beginning of the sixteenth century onwards
has been slowly rising to dominance within the European races.
I mean that trend to free, unfettered, individual activity in crafts-

manship, in agriculture, and in all mercantile transactions. The
culmination of this epoch, with its trend still in this direction,
can be roughly assigned to the stretch of time from the middle
of the eighteenth century to the middle of the nineteenth century. During that hundred years the populations in Europe and
America suffered many evils from want, starvation and war.
These evils have always afflicted mankind in the mass. Within
this period one essential quality stimulated all sociological func-
tionings.

That quality was hope—not the hope of ignorance. The peculiar character of this central period was that the wise men
hoped, and that as yet no circumstance had arisen to throw
doubt upon the grounds of such hope. The chief seats of economic, and of general sociological, speculation were in France
and Great Britain. The realized trend towards individualism,
and away from mediaevalism, had vastly simplified the problem
of constructing a social theory which should correspond to the
practical ideal of civilized life when relieved from the madness
of its traditional rulers, Kings, Priests, and Nobles. For nearly
three hundred years before the middle of the eighteenth century,
a continual process of simplification in practice and in theory
had prevailed. Feudalism was in full decay, the complex interweaving of church authority with secular government was stead-
ily vanishing. Society could be conceived as functioning in terms
of the friendly competition of its individual members, with the
State standing as umpire in the minority of instances when there
occurred a breakdown of these normal relations.

Primarily this competition of activities concerned the production of material goods for the support of physical life. As to other
values, the later formula of "A Free Church in a Free State"
sufficed. There the word "Church" suggests religion. But it was

in practice extended to all organizations for the supply of every variety of nonmaterial values, religious, aesthetic, moral, including the natural feelings of human affection. I am endeavoring to sketch to you the perfect doctrine of an individualistic society, which was naively presupposed in sociological theorizing from the midst of the eighteenth century to that of the nineteenth. The doctrines were never realized in their full purity. But all social progress was in the direction which they indicated. These doctrines were more perfectly realized in America than elsewhere. But they also admirably fitted themselves to the needs of the commercial middle classes in England, France, and wherever in Europe this middle class was a chief factor in the social life. The American Revolution and the French Revolution were dramatic incidents arising from the acceptance of this sociology. The reconstruction of Europe after the Napoleonic Wars was guided by it. Also, it was evidently the fact that life was healthier, finer, more upstanding, in proportion to the dominance of this social individualism.

In respect to this doctrine, Where do we stand today? I will not quote from any theorist indulging in brilliant speculation. I will take a sentence from the editorial page of one of the leading Boston newspapers, in its current issue which has been placed by my side as I write. Here is the judgment of this organ of Boston commercial opinion—"Whether we fancy it or not, we are in the midst of a revolution, so far as concerns the relation of the individual to the Federal Government."

Evidently something has happened. The pure milk of the word of the sociological Gospel, perfected in the late eighteenth century, has gone sour.

Undoubtedly, during the central period the Gospel of Individualism was working well wherever it was tried. But only in

North America was it ever the wholly dominant fact. In Europe, it always had the aspect of a new mode of sociological functioning gradually superseding the relics of an antecedent order. This older layer of law and custom had somewhat the air of a deposit of rubbish, in process of removal. Perhaps this aspect was partly a mistake. The relics of the older order may have been providing for the realization of a diversity of values which the pure practice of the new sociology would have left unsatisfied. I will return to this point later.

In America very special conditions for human life were at that time in full operation. An empty continent, peculiarly well suited for European races, was in process of occupation. Also that section of these races which felt the urge towards that type of human adventure had freely selected itself to constitute the American population devoted to this enterprise. Accordingly, in America this epoch exhibits a wonderful development of sturdy independence, with the individual members of the population freely carving out their own destinies. This is the Epic Epoch of American life, and after the initial struggles of small beginnings it had a wonderful central period of about a hundred and fifty to two hundred years. It was a triumph of individual freedom, for those who liked that sort of opportunity. And the population was largely selected by its own or its ancestral urge towards exactly that sort of life. Indeed the evil side of the survivals of feudalism in European life is illustrated by the bitter feelings which lingered amid the recollections and traditions of the American population. This episode in human existence, when individualism dominated American life, cannot be too closely studied by sociologists. It is the only instance where large masses of civilized mankind have enjoyed a regime of unqualified individualism, unfettered by law or custom.

THE NEW FORCES AT WORK—THE PASSING
OF INDIVIDUALISM

From the middle of the nineteenth century, new forces have been at work, and gradually the situation both in Europe and America has been changed. Up to that time, for nearly two centuries human progress had been identified with the advance of individualism. In England, the Industrial Revolution had been in operation for about seventy years, and in America and Continental Europe for a somewhat shorter period. Its first effect had been to promote the sturdy individualism of the middle classes. It enriched them and stimulated their energy. It destroyed the decaying elements of the past. About a hundred years ago two Englishmen were leaning on the balustrade of a railway bridge, watching a railway train pass under them. This was a novel sight in those days. "It is an ugly thing," said one of them, "but it is the death of Feudalism." The speaker was a strong advocate of the liberal individualism characteristic of that epoch. He did not foresee that in another two generations the new mechanism would send the then existing Individualism into the same grave with the old Feudalism.

Of this trilogy, Feudalism, Individualism, Ugliness, today the Ugliness alone survives, a living threat to the values of life.

The recent phase of modern industrialism has been produced by a change of scale in industrial operations. One of the dangerous fallacies in the construction of scientific theory is to make observations upon one scale of magnitude and to translate their results into laws valid for another scale. Almost always some large modification is required, and an entire inversion of fundamental conceptions may be necessary. For example, on a large scale of observation there are bits of matter, such as rocks, tables, lumps of iron, solid, resistant, immobile. On another, microscopic, scale there are a welter of molecules in ceaseless activity and each molecule only definable in terms of such activity. The physical science of the two preceding centuries made exactly this mistake. It naively transferred principles derived from its large-scale observations to apply to the operations of nature within the minute scale of individual atoms. I suggest that our sociological doctrines have made the same error in the opposite direction as to scales. We argue from small-scale relations between humans, say two men and a boy on a desert island, to the theory of the relations of the great commercial organizations either with the general public or internally with their own personnel. In any one corporation we may have to consider tens of thousands of employees, hundreds of executives, scores of directors, scores of thousands of owners, and a few controlling financial magnates in the background. I am not saying that such corporations are undesirable. That is not my belief. Indeed, such organizations are necessary for our modern type of civilization. But I do say that observations of the behaviours of two men and a boy on a desert island, or of the inhabitants of a small country village, have very little to do with the sociology of our modern type of industrial civilization.

In any large city, almost everyone is an employee, employing his working hours in exact ways predetermined by others. Even his manners may be prescribed. So far as sheer individual freedom is concerned, there was more diffused freedom in the City of London in the year 1633, when Charles the First was King, than there is today in any industrial city of the world.

It is impossible to understand the social history of our ancestors unless we remember the surging freedom which then existed within the cities, of England, of Flanders, of the Rhine Valley, and of Northern Italy. Under our present industrial system, this type of freedom is being lost. This loss means the fading from human life of values infinitely precious to it. The divergent urges of different individual temperaments can no longer find their various satisfactions in serious activities. There only remain iron-bound conditions of employment and trivial amusements for leisure. I suggest that one subject of our study for our industrial and sociological statesmen should be the preservation of freedom for those who are engaged in mass production and mass distribution which are necessities in our modern civilization. It is a study requiring penetrating insight so as to distinguish between the realities of freedom and its mere show, and between hurtful and fruitful ways of freedom.

My point is that the change of scale in modern industry has made nearly the whole of previous literature on the topic irrelevant, and indeed mischievous. The study requires deep consideration of the various values for human life. I am not suggesting any facile solution. The topic is very perplexing. It involves many branches of psychology—general psychology, industrial psychology, and mass psychology. It involves sociological and political theory. It involves the role of aesthetics in human contentment. It involves an estimate of the sense of effectiveness aroused by cooperation in enterprises with large aims. It involves the understanding of physiological requirements. It involves presuppositions, however dim, as to the aims of human life. But above all, and beyond all, it involves direct observation and practical experience. Unless the twentieth century can produce a whole body of reasoned literature elucidating the many aspects of this great topic, it will go hard with the civilization that we love.

THE INCREASING PRESSURE OF GENERAL UNEMPLOYMENT

I now turn to another consideration which cannot be separated from the previous topic. The dangers to freedom are largely cloaked in times of prosperity by the scarcity of labor. In such times, at least the desire for change can be satisfied. If one job does not suit, a man can try another. If the type of work remains the same, at least there is a change of factory, or overseers, and of associates. The real cause for restlessness may lie deeper, but something has happened. Also the scarcity of labor affects the mentality of the management.

In a time of widespread unemployment this outlet for discontent is closed. A man is lucky if he be not in the bread line. There is a very real closing down of freedom for everyone concerned, from the higher executives to the lowest grade of employees. In any industrial district in the world today, it is a grim joke to speak of freedom. All that remains is the phantasm of freedom, devoid of opportunity.

It is therefore of the first importance to have in our minds some estimate of the probable frequency of these periods when there is an excess of labor. In England, where long ago any pioneering period has ceased, this excess of labor is almost normal. Sometimes it is more so, and sometimes less. But for more than a hundred years—indeed from the time of Queen Elizabeth —the out-of-work problem has been always there. There are reasons why this evil should settle on the whole industrial world as a permanent factor in life, unless the great corporations can adapt their mode of functioning. Up to now the problem has been mitigated by the existence of empty continents in the temperate zones. This relief has vanished.

The combination of mass production and of technological improvement secures that more and more standardized goods can be produced by fewer and fewer workers. Here and there there are mitigating causes. But the general fact remains, ever advancing in importance. The issue is unemployment. The proper phrase is "technological unemployment." But you do not get rid of a grim fact by the use of a technical term. The result is that a portion of the population can supply the standardized necessaries of life, and the first luxuries, for the whole population. A portion of the population will be idle, and as time goes on, this portion will grow larger.

In the second place, the demand for goods grows slack. This is to be expected. For the idle, or the partially idle, cannot afford to be brisk buyers. Thus the full quota of goods for the whole population is not wanted, and so again there is another reason for unemployment.

These two grounds for dullness of trade are often cloaked by other agencies with a contrary effect. They stay, however, permanently in the background, a constant aggravation of any trade depression, and a constant provocation of bitter discontent.

The Mistaken Policy of Modern Salesmanship and Production

Beyond these effects, the modern salesmanship associated with mass production is producing a more deep-seated reason for the insecurity of trade. We are witnessing a determined attempt to canalize the aesthetic enjoyments of the population. A certain broad canalization is, of course, necessary. Apart from large uniformities, all effort is ineffective. But all intensity of enjoyment, sustained with the strength of individual character, arises from the individual taste diversifying the stream of uniformity. Destroy individuality, and you are left with a vacancy of aesthetic feeling, drifting this way and that, with vague satisfactions and vague discontents.

This destruction is produced by the determined attempt to force completely finished standardized products upon the buyers. The whole motive appealed to is conformation to a standard fashion and not individual satisfaction with the individual thing. The result must be the creation of a public with feeble individual tastes. There is nothing that they really want to buy, unless the world around them is also buying. This is an admirable condition for mass buying when the times are favorable. But it is an equally effective condition for mass abstention from buying when expenditure is once checked. The stimulus of the individual want for the individual thing has been destroyed. And after all, individual buyers have to buy individual things.

Thus large oscillations in demand arise from comparatively slight causes. The sturdy individuality of the mass of the public is the greatest security for steadiness in trade. It is this individuality that the great commercial corporations are setting themselves to destroy. Independent individuality of demand is the tacit presupposition of much of the older political economy. Thus, whether we survey the producers or the buyers, we find the same steady decay of individuality. Now, a decay of individuality finally means the gradual vanishing of aesthetic preferences as effective factors in social behaviours. The aesthetic capacities of the producers and the aesthetic cravings of the buyers are losing any real effectiveness. The canalization of the whole range of industry is in rapid progress. Apart from the dangers of economic prosperity, there is in this decay a loss to happiness.

Varied feelings are fading out. We are left with generalized mass emotion.

My line of argument up to this point is not the preliminary to an attack on great commercial corporations. These organizations are the first stage of a new and beneficent social structure. My complaint is that in the two or three generations of their existence on their present scale, they have functioned much too simply. They should enlarge the scope of their activities. To understand what is required, we should ask why France stands out as a tremendous exception to the general sociological trend. She has preserved the individuality of her craftsmanship and the individuality of her aesthetic appreciations. This is the secret of the undying vitality of the French nation. What I suggest is that the great corporations in various ways should interweave in their organizations individual craftsmanship operating upon the products of their mass production. For example, take the most obvious of all the aesthetic products in the world today, namely, the dress of women. If you enter a leading Boston store today, you are lucky if you find material illustrating as many as five shades of blue. The other shades are out of fashion. Such is the decree of the business world. Delicate craftsmanship, subtle combinations, individualities of taste are out of the question. Today the world of women is restricted to the fashionable blue. Subtlety of taste is ruthlessly stamped out. In this example, the delicacies of craftsmanship are irrelevant to the operations of the great producing firms.

Of course, mass production underlies the modern standards of life. What we require is a close interweaving of the two forms of activity, the production of the general material and the perfection of the individual thing. Of course there are all sorts of half-way houses. I can only here state my meaning in crude outline. The great producers and the great distributing corporations should include in their activities the work of craftsmen and designers.

THE NEED FOR ECONOMIC STATESMANSHIP

This concerns another point relating to our present troubles. We are told that the seat of the evil is our distribution of goods. In its more obvious sense this doctrine is certainly wrong. The organization for the delivery of goods to any purchasers could hardly be more perfect, whether we think of the neighborhood of a town, or of the whole of America, or of the whole of the civilized world. What is at fault is that for the majority of people the ability to procure goods depends upon the exercise of some useful activity. But mass production has restricted the quantity of human activity required. Hence a large number of people are unable to procure goods. But when we look at France, we see that we have wantonly suppressed a very considerable side of human activity, for which large numbers of human beings are admirably fitted. The result is that we have both suppressed the opportunity for self-expression which is so necessary for happiness, and have extinguished the claim of a large section of people upon the goods which lie ready for consumption.

What is defective is not distribution, but the variety of opportunity for useful activity. Thus the interweaving of mass production with craftsmanship should be the supreme object of economic statesmanship. Here by craftsmanship I do not mean the exact reproduction of types of activity belonging to the past. I mean the evolution of such types of individual design and of individual procedure as are proper for the crude material which lies ready for fashioning into particular products.

Also I must avoid another misconception. Nothing that I am

saying has any reference to any action now desirable for the rescue of the world from its present state of miserable depression. Such action must be immediate and must therefore presuppose the existing modes of economic activity. I am speaking of the tasks awaiting economic statesmanship during the next twenty-five years. My point is that in our economic system as now developed there is a starvation of human impulses, a denial of opportunity, a limitation of beneficial activity—in short, a lack of freedom. I have endeavored to show that this fault in our system produces in various ways an excess of irritability in the social organism. Whatever system we have, the natural fluctuations of the universe will produce in it ups and downs, from better to worse. But this irritability latent in our present modes of functioning seizes hold of these fluctuations and exaggerates them. These recurrent depressions have been growing more and more dangerous and are likely to grow worse. In our search for remedies, we must consider the things that cannot be reduced to machinery, things material and things spiritual. Again, the present argument is only a putting together of considerations which have already been developed by others. In fact, much of this discussion is a commonplace of literature. More than a hundred years ago, Southey pointed out the destruction of beauty in the lives of the operatives in the manufacturing districts of England. In the third quarter of the nineteenth century Ruskin was denouncing the absence of aesthetic values in the English industrial system. Both Southey and Ruskin were fantastic and impracticable, but they fastened attention upon a real blot. Relevantly to the present situation, Professor Ames of Dartmouth has expounded with great insight the case of interweaving aesthetic activities in the leisure provided by mechanized mass production. Also at Harvard, Professor Mayo and his band of workers have made a notable advance in the analysis of industrial psychology. In the combination of these points of views, we have the foundation for a new chapter in Economic Statesmanship.

THE EDUCATIONAL PROBLEM

This conclusion has a moral for education. A training in handicraft of all types should form a large element in every curriculum. Education is not merely an appeal to the abstract intelligence. Purposeful activity, intellectual activity, and the immediate sense of worth-while achievement, should be conjoined in a unity of experience. Of course, this doctrine must be worked with discretion, and in proportion to the other necessities of education. At the latest state of education, namely in university life, a differentiation takes place. A large proportion of the students should devote themselves to sheer intellectual training. But in Science, in Technology, and in Art, a large infusion of hand work should be a serious element in the work of a considerable section of the students. My own experience, which is a large one, in the educational requirements of the population in London has convinced me that the sharp distinction between institutions devoted to abstract knowledge and those devoted to application and to handicraft is a mistake. Every university will have its emphasis, this way or that. But I see no advantage in an anxious drawing of an exact line of demarcation. The mass of mankind, including many of its most valuable leaders, requires something betwixt and between. Common sense and no abstract theory should dictate what any particular university attempts.

This doctrine is most easily exemplified in the sphere of the fine arts, though, of course, craftsmanship is not limited to artistic production. Industry and art alike will be on a healthier basis when the natural avenue to fine art is through craftsmanship with the cultivation of fine sensibility. In addition to the general design of the mass-made product, there can also be interwoven possibilities of adding individual differentiation to individual things. The finer genius can develop into the specialized artist with his work abstracted from all association with other utility.

In conclusion, it is obvious that any blending of a machine age with a vigorous craftsmanship will require a large cooperation between schools and universities and the great business interests concerned with production and distribution. It will also require the education of the general public. It will require the advice of technologists of all types from engineers to artists. It will destroy much of the sweet simplicity of modern business policy which fastens its attention solely on one aspect of our complex human nature. But if it can be accomplished it will add to the happiness of mankind, notably so by stabilizing the popular requirements and widening the area of useful occupations.

III

Memories

I

A WAY of life is something more than the shifting relations of bits of matter in space and in time. Life depends upon such external facts. The all-important aesthetic rises out of them, and is deflected by them. But, in abstraction from the atmosphere of feeling, one behavior pattern is as good as another; and they are all equally uninteresting. The chief value of memories of infancy and young childhood is that with unconscious naiveté they convey the tonality of the society amid which that childhood was passed. The two generations immediately preceding the present time are so near and so far. We can almost hear the rustle of their clothes as they passed away in the shades. The tones of their voices, their ways of approach, linger. And yet the generation on the younger side of fifty knows so little of them. The blatant emphasis of current literature has done its worst in distortion. Memories shed a quiet light upon ways of feeling which in literature become distorted for the necessities of a story, or of a comparison.

In the autumn of 1864 a small boy three years old was in Paris. He was, however, unconscious of date, of reason, and of

79

personal age. The very notion of the great world of tremendous happenings was absent from his mind. He enjoyed as matter of course the love and petting from the family of parents, children, nurse, and the bright warm days. But one baffling, elusive memory remained throughout life, a thread connecting the child with the onrush of history.

The scene was a bright day, the nurse sitting on a seat facing a broad road, the child playing, a park with its beauty of trees and flowers and shrubs, a palace from which the road came; and whither the road went the child neither knew nor cared. Along the road a glittering regiment of soldiers marched from the palace, and, passing the seat, vanished into the unknown. That was the whole scene, disconnected from any background of date or place, and yet haunting memory in later years. Throughout boyhood he tried again and again to identify the spot. Each year for two months in the late spring he was living in a London house looking across Green Park toward Buckingham Palace. He knew every seat that faced the roads where companies of Queen Victoria's Guards marched to and fro from the palace. The Queen herself, as she drove past, was a familiar sight—a little figure in black, belonging to the unquestioned order of the universe, but at that time, toward the end of the decade of the eighteen-sixties, too retired to be very popular. But the seat of his dream, with its company of soldiers marching from a palace toward the unknown, remained undiscovered.

Years later, in the summer of 1880, I was again in Paris, with my two elder brothers, one of them a schoolmaster, the other a tutor at Oxford. Again as at the former time, we were returning from Switzerland. Scenes of infancy were entirely out of our thoughts. We were returning to work—the work of the master at an ancient school, of the tutor at Trinity College, Oxford, and of the freshman at Trinity College, Cambridge. We were young men immersed in the academic life of England. The future, like the dream road from the palace to the unknown, lay before us. But suddenly, as I stood in the gardens of the Tuileries, I found the very place of my dreams. The seat was there; the road was there; and the park was there. The dream that had haunted boyhood was discovered to be a reality held in memory.

The vision of the child had caught a glimpse of the pageant of history, and again the second vision gave the tragic interpretation. The palace now stood a ruin, with its charred walls. The Emperor, Napoleon III, had died an exile in England. The road led to Sedan, and the gallant regiments of the French Empire had marched to their doom. The final act of the Napoleonic drama, for which during eighty years Europe was the stage— this final phase, at the glitter of its height and in its downfall, had been flashed upon me in two visions of a seat, a palace, and a road.

At the time of the first vision to the child playing in the garden, secure within his own small world of feelings, human life was exhibiting every diverse phase of horror, enjoyment, and ambition. On September 2, 1864, Atlanta was occupied by the Union forces, and almost immediately Sherman submitted to Grant his plan for his march from Atlanta to the sea—at the very time when the child was playing in the garden. Bismarck was perfecting the policy which brought about the overthrow of Austria within two years. Italy was waiting to seize Rome. The Pope was consolidating his control over the Church, to balance his loss of temporal power. England was nearing the end of the second of its only two long periods of complete security, after the defeat of

Louis XIV and after the defeat of Napoleon. Each period was marked by the dominance of a small group of liberal aristocrats.

II

But the history of the world is not focused in any one life. Lincoln had one experience, and his fellow countrymen had each their own experience. The great events that historians speak of influenced more or less directly the lives of all men. But the stuff of human life cannot be wholly construed in terms of historical events; it mainly consists of feelings arising from reactions between small definite groups of persons.

For this reason the generalized history of an epoch sadly misrepresents the real individual feelings of the quiet people in back streets and in country towns. For example, the Victorian epoch in England as seen from our present standpoint entirely misrepresents my memories of the tone of thought of quiet, moderately prosperous people at a time round about the year 1870. I am not talking of agitators, or of people harboring grievances, but of the ordinary type of leading citizen in a quiet country town. I have already said that the Queen was not popular, and her sanity was doubted. Later she was canonized; but that time was not yet. Also the Prince of Wales, later King Edward the Seventh, was then frankly disliked. The Princess of Wales was beautiful, kindly, and spotless in her conduct; but this only added fuel to the fire as stories passed around. I remember definitely hearing the talk of my elders, that if the Queen died there would have to be a Republic.

From that date the Queen rapidly recovered influence. She became an institution, a legend. Her very individuality, which in the middle period of her reign had annoyed, toward the end became the subject of pride. She was no namby-pamby person who courted popularity. But the Prince of Wales was lucky in the survival of his mother. About twenty years later, in 1890, for a short time he could not appear in public without the escort of the Princess of Wales to subdue the hisses and the ribald shouts. There had been some gambling scandals. But the history of England in the nineteenth century represents a loyal nation gathered lovingly round a spotless throne.

I lived in circles where, if anywhere, loyalty would be found. What really stabilized England was a relatively small group of aristocrats of liberal opinions. These men were highly respected, and had no intention of allowing the country to drift toward any useless experiments. For this reason the desertion of the reforming party by these men over the question of Irish Home Rule, in 1886, was a fatal blow at the old political habits of England.

As to the way in which these men, at the height of their power, managed the Throne, I have been told this story by the son of a cabinet minister who witnessed the incident. During one of Mr. Gladstone's ministries there was a crisis in foreign affairs. The Queen vehemently objected to the policy of the Liberal Cabinet. For a whole series of cabinet meetings, Mr. Gladstone opened the proceedings by extracting from his dispatch case, with immense solemnity, a letter from the Queen, a new one each time. With growing solemnity, and with all the aid of his magnificent voice, he slowly read Her Majesty's letter. The group of aristocrats who formed the Ministry leaned forward with marked attention to catch every word which emanated from the monarch. The letter always consisted of vehement reproaches to the Ministry for the folly of their conduct. The letter finished, Mr. Gladstone solemnly replaced the document in his dispatch case. The Cabinet then proceeded to business without one word of allusion to the letter, either then or to each other afterward. And the policy of the ministers was never deflected by a hairsbreadth. I doubt if any modern English group of ministers could behave in this way, so inflexibly and with such restraint. But that was the way in which the Whigs ruled the country. In England to-day there is no coherent body of this sort.

This story of Queen Victoria and a group of well-trained politicians is very trivial. It belongs to the frippery of government: how to deal with an awkward incident, of which the importance was more social than political. But the interest is to notice how a score of men with a certain sort of training do in fact deal with such situations. It belongs to the art of preventing minor difficulties from growing into great crises.

It is curious how detached incidents remain in memory. I can vividly remember the old bobbin man who supplied my parents' household with kindling for the coal fires during the first half of the eighteen-seventies. I expect that these bobbins ought to have been called "fagots," but in the villages of East Kent we called them "bobbins." He was a curious old man, completely without education and earning a scanty living. He was dressed in corduroys, of an antiquity defying any exact estimate of date. He cut the scrub undergrowth in the woods near Canterbury, about seventeen miles away from us. He then chopped the wood into the required lengths, and tied the sticks up into parcels—each parcel, or bobbin, being about the amount required to light a fire. He came through the village about once a fortnight, or once in three weeks, with a large cart piled high with bobbins. As he passed, he called out, "Bobbins! Bobbins!" in a curious, harshly rhythmical voice which stays in memory after more than half a century.

The horse was even more decrepit than the man—an old, wornout cart horse. The pace of the procession was about one and three-quarter miles an hour. They—the man walking beside the horse—plodded along, unresting and untiring, so near their end and yet seemingly timeless and eternal. He, his horse, Queen Victoria, and her cabinet ministers, all belong to the essential stuff of English History. So does my father, the thoroughly countrified vicar of the parish, as I can now see him half a century ago chatting to the old bobbin man. They were on very friendly terms. Unfortunately only one fragment of their conversation survives. It was the old bobbin man who said: "There are some as goes rootling and tearing about. But, Lor'bless you, sir, I gets to Saturday night as soon as any of'em." That is an authentic bit of village speech, nigh sixty years ago, and the speakers have all passed into their final Saturday night, together with their whole world of ways of life.

III

While on the topic of life in a country vicarage, another visual memory flashes upon me: there is an Archbishop of Canterbury, tall, commanding, stately. He is in a genial mood, with his back to the bright fire in the ample hall of the old vicarage house. He is laughing heartily as my father tells him of the theology of the leading parishioner, who found great comfort in the doctrine of eternal damnation. That incident is also sixty years since. The Archbishop and the leading parishioner must be added to the group of those who make up the stuff of English History.

That Archbishop remains in my memory as one of the few great men whom I have met. I mean men with outstanding governing force conjoined with capacious intellect. I do not think that he was subtle; but there was no doubt about him. Archbishop Tait ought to have been a prime minister. Fate made him Archbishop of Canterbury. I have always been grateful for my glimpse

of him during half-a-dozen years, and for the family tradition
of him during a longer period. To have seen Tait was worth
shelves of volumes of mediaeval history. He magnificently closed
the line of great ecclesiastics who organized the intimate cultural life of England, round monasteries, village churches, dio-
ceses, cathedrals, parishes—in New England called "townships"
—parish meetings, schools, colleges, universities. The line
stretches from Augustine of Canterbury, through Theodore of
Tarsus, Lanfranc, Anselm, Becket, Warham, Cranmer, Parker,
Laud, Sancroft, Tillotson, Tait. The national activities that cluster
round the archbishops as representative leaders, are as much
worth dwelling on as those that centre round kings and parlia-
ments.

Tait really closed the line in the sense in which I am thinking.
All these men from Augustine to Tait energetically acted on
the policy that the Church was the national organ to foster the
intimate, ultimate values which enter into human life. For the
earlier men, the Church was more than that; but at least it was
that. They refused to conceive the Church as merely one party
within the nation, or merely as one factor within civilization. For
them the Church was the nation rising to the height of its civilization. They were men with vision—wide, subtle, magnificent.
They failed. Tait was the last Archbishop who effectively sustained the policy. Since his time, English ecclesiastical policy has
been directed to organizing the Anglican Church as a special
group within the nation.

But the failure of the earlier set of men was a magnificent one.
Their policy prevailed for twelve hundred years. It civilized
Europe. Country after country has discarded it as an archaic ob-
struction. Even to-day, Spain and Mexico are engaged in casting
it away. The interest of men like Warham, Parker, Tillotson,

Tait, is that they rescued the final stage of the mediaeval vision of civilization from the reproach of decrepit reaction. Its end in Spain at the present moment is that of a backward-looking system, divorced from modern realities. Its supporters in Spain are mediaeval, blind and deaf to the modern world. But Tait, Tillotson, and Warham, each in his day, were forward-looking men. They took the inherited notion of cultural organization, and tried to give it a new life in terms of the modern world. They failed. Tait was the last of the line. Since his time, smaller men have drifted along with limited aims. Their aims are quite sensible, granting their belief. But they completely fail to stir the blood of those who seek for a vision of civilization in this world.

Perhaps men like Warham, Tillotson, and Tait had gone back behind Christianity to the ideals of Pericles. But to-day, when we are blindly groping for some coherent ordering of civilization, we can spare some sympathy for the men who in England tried to give new life to the old vision which for twelve hundred years had served Europe so well. In England the death of the old ideal had a nobility worthy of its services during its long life.

IV

To return to my theme of memories, we left the Archbishop standing on the vicarage hearthrug, laughing at the silly old gentleman who consoled himself with the thought of the eternal torture of his neighbors.

I can remember the old gentleman well. He was not at all cruel, but simply, incredibly silly. The Archbishop also knew him well, and that is why the religious aspect did not, at the moment, strike him.

Another picture of the old gentleman rises before me. He was taking the chair at a penny reading in the parish schoolroom, which in the evenings acted as an entertainment hall. A penny reading was a series of readings of extracts from good literature— or, at least, what was supposed to be good literature. For the humorous and pathetic pieces Dickens was the favorite author; and among the works of Dickens *Pickwick* was the chief favorite for the comic relief. A certain amount of romantic poetry also was a necessary part—usually Sir Walter Scott. One man did all the reading, someone to whom the parish looked for light and leading in literary matters. For example, a clergyman from a neighboring parish, or a doctor, or a lawyer; in fact, someone whom the villagers would like to look at for an hour and a half. The entertainment cost a penny, as the name implies. The proceeds about paid for the cost of the gas and of the caretaker. Their entertainer was repaid by a supper at the vicarage and a vote of thanks proposed by my father, who usually took the chair. Also I forgot to mention two or three songs, solos, with piano accompaniment, which came between the selections read, and gave the reader a rest. We only rarely rose to a violin solo.

These penny readings spread to every village in southern England at that time. I know nothing about the North of England so far as concerns the details of its life. In the South we were fully occupied with our own village lives. We took no interest in the North of England, which manufactured our linen and woolen clothes; no interest in France, whose cliffs we could see on every fine evening; nor in North America, whose epic of development was the greatest contemporary fact in human history. I am not defending the country folk of East Kent. Facts are stubborn, and it is my present business to state them as I remember.

On the evening in question, my father was the reader at the village penny reading. So the silly old gentleman, as the leading resident, was asked to take the chair. I see him now as though it were yesterday, rising at the close of the meeting, hemming and hawing: "The vicar—has asked me—to thank him—for his great kindness—in so ably entertaining us—and amusing us—this evening." He then had gained his sea legs, and ended quite fluently: "And so, in reponse to his request, I ask you to join me in thanking him for this magnificent entertainment." On the whole, what he said was the mere truth. But it illustrates how necessary is a decent reserve in the ceremonial of social life.

The penny readings were the first faint signs of a revolution in English culture. Its accomplishment took about fifty years. The England of the eighteenth century and of the main part of the nineteenth century consisted of a highly educated upper class composed of landowners, leaders in business and commerce, and professional men. But the great mass of manual laborers, of artisans, and of the lower end of the traders, were very deficiently educated, if at all. After the middle of the century, and more especially after the first move toward democracy in 1868, the education of the whole nation was seriously initiated. "Let us educate our masters!" exclaimed a leading statesman in a speech in the House of Commons when the plunge had been taken. Of course the movement was slow in getting under way, and still slower in producing any visible effect. But now, looking across fifty or sixty years of conscious recollection, I can see that schools and universities have produced an entirely new type of Englishman, so far as concerns the mass of people.

The standard comments on English education of the earlier period were contained in the Essays of Matthew Arnold. At the time when he wrote they were true enough. But nothing in his Essays applies to the England of to-day. It is still fashionable for superior persons in England to quote him as though his criticisms still applied. But these superior persons are engrossed in reading literature and often have scanty knowledge of the immediate facts around them. One of my most precious memories is that I have, within the space of my lifetime, witnessed the education of England, and the change in English lives that that education has meant.

V

The old bobbin man, as he journeyed with his horse and wagon slowly from the woods near Canterbury to the North Foreland at the tip of Kent, passed through scenes of English History unthinkingly and unknowingly. There still remain in England individuals of his mental grade. But as a type he has vanished from the land. The gap in education between classes has been largely closed. To him the immense story of Canterbury, with its relics of martyrs, heroes, artists, and kings, was as nothing. He jogged along across the meadow marshland with Roman forts on either hand; he passed through the village of Minster, with its magnificent Norman church and its relics of a monastery that once ruled the neighborhood; he saw the spot where Saint Augustine preached his first sermon; he saw the beach where the Saxons landed; he passed Osengal—that is, the place of bones—perhaps the first English graveyard. But all these things were as nothing to him. He could appreciate neither the past from which he sprung nor the forces of the present which so soon were to sweep away folk like him.

The age of a vast subject population, deaf and dumb to the values belonging to civilization, has gone. Also the old civilizing influence of the Church has passed. It has been replaced by secular schools, colleges, universities, and by the activities of the men and women on their faculties. In the age to come, how will these new agencies compare with the ecclesiastics, the monks, the nuns, and the friars, who brought their phase of civilization to Western Europe?

At the present time, the system of modern universities has reached its triumphant culmination. They cover all civilized lands, and the members of their faculties control knowledge and its sources. The old system also enjoyed its triumph. From the seventh to the thirteenth century, it also decisively altered the mentalities of the surrounding populations. Men could not endow monasteries or build cathedrals quickly enough. Without doubt they hoped to save their souls; but the merits of their gifts would not have been evident unless there had been a general feeling of the services to the surrounding populations performed by these religious foundations. Then, when we pass over another two centuries, and watch the men about the year fifteen hundred, we find an ominous fact. These foundations, which started with such hope and had performed such services, were in full decay. Men like Erasmus could not speak of them without an expression of contempt. Europe endured a hundred years of revolution in order to shake off the system. Men such as Warham, and Tillotson, and Tait struggled for another three centuries to maintain it in a modified form. But they too have failed. With this analogy in mind, we wonder what in a hundred years, or in two hundred years, will be the fate of the modern university system which now is triumphant in its mission of civilization. We should search to remove the seeds of decay. We cannot be more secure now than was the ecclesiastical system at the end of the twelfth century and for a century onward. And it failed.

To my mind our danger is exactly the same as that of the older system. Unless we are careful, we shall conventionalize knowledge. Our literary criticism will suppress initiative. Our historical criticism will conventionalize our ideas of the springs of human conduct. Our scientific systems will suppress all understanding of the ways of the universe which fall outside their abstractions. Our modes of testing ability will exclude all the youth whose ways of thought lie outside our conventions of learning. In such ways the universities, with their scheme of orthodoxies, will stifle the progress of the race, unless by some fortunate stirring of humanity they are in time remodeled or swept away. These are our dangers, as yet only to be seen on the distant horizon, clouds small as the hand of a man.

Those of us who have lived for seventy years, more or less, have seen first the culmination of an epoch, and then its disruption and decay. What is happening when an epoch approaches its culmination? What is happening as it passes toward its decay? Historical writing is cursed with simple characterizations of great events. Historians should study zoology. Naturalists tell us that in the background of our animal natures we harbor the traces of the earlier stages of our animal race. Theologians tell us that we are nerved to effort by the distant vision of ideals, claiming realization. Both sets are right. A daughter of John Addington Symonds, in a novel entitled *A Child of the Alps,* remarks: "Spring is not a season, it is a battleground between summer and winter."

In like manner every active epoch harbors within itself the ideals and the ways of its immediate predecessors. An epoch is a complex fact; and in many of its departments these inherited modes of thought and custom survive, unshaken and dominant. But on the whole the modes of the past are recessive, sinking into an unexpressed background. They are still there, giving a tonality to all that happens, and capable of flaring into a transient outburst when aroused by some touch of genius. Nor is it true that these vanishing ways of thought only appeal to the more backward natures. On the contrary, we find men of capacious intellect and cautious natures endeavoring, in this way and in that way, to adapt the wealth of inheritance to the oncoming fashions of thought. That is how I characterized some of the outstanding Archbishops of Canterbury, from Warham to Tait. Such men disagree in many ways. For example, Tillotson and Tait stand in sharp antagonism to Laud. But they all agree in that they were endeavoring to adapt some generalization of the old ecclesiastical-feudal organization of mankind to the purposes of the dominant rationalistic-individualistic epoch.

We were apt to conceive the Puritans who in the first half of the seventeenth century founded the Commonwealth of Massachusetts as the direct antagonists of these men. But, as we now know, this is a complete mistake. These Puritans were endeavoring to carry over a remodeled ecclesiastical organization as a dominant institution in the new individualistic epoch. In many ways these Puritans are to be classed with Laud, as striving to preserve more of the old world than either Tillotson or Tait.

The true antithesis to all these men is Roger Williams. Curiously enough, this man, who more completely than any other expressed the new individualistic tendencies, seems to stand as an isolated rebel, outside his own times, and yet not fitting into the world of either of the centuries subsequent to his own. He embodied too completely the dominant features of the oncoming world.

In the last seventy years this individualism culminated, retaining as a background the monarchical, aristocratic social ways. These social ways were the recessive retention of the old feudal ecclesiastical system of the Middle Ages. We have watched these ways fading away into the undiscernible inheritance of the past. All that we can now see of them consists of funny little relics here and there—reminding one of the Lion and the Unicorn on the old Boston State House. But with this final triumph of individualism the whole epoch crumbled. New methods of coordination are making their appearance as yet not understood. These principles of organization are based upon economic necessities. That is about all we know of them; the rest is controversy. The older principles of the mediaeval system were derived from religious aspirations. Undoubtedly we have lost color in the foreground by this shift from the ideal to the practical; but the change is more in appearance than in fact. The practical was always there —the hard routine by which the folk of the mediaeval times barely sustained life. The difference is that nature controlled them, while we now see our way to the control of nature. That is why the topic of production, distribution, and the organization of labor is now in the foreground.

The other side—the shift in the prominence of the religious motive in social organization—that is too large a topic for the end of a paper.

IV

England and the Narrow Seas

I

IN English records of the sixteenth and seventeenth centuries there is a phrase which often recurs—"the Narrow Seas." Historians treat it as a name, and tell us, rightly enough, that it refers to the seas which lie just north and south of the Straits of Dover. But what they do not tell us adequately is how greatly the fate of the world has been affected by the peculiarities of these narrow seas. The marked character of these seas has impressed itself upon the populations on its shores: in England these are the East Kent folk and East Anglians from Essex, Suffolk, Norfolk, and Lincolnshire; and on the continent across the water they are the people of the Low Countries—namely, Holland, Belgium, and the north-western coast of France. There are two characteristics impressed on all these populations, with the possible exception of the French section, which has for its hinterland the Latin influence of France. These characteristics are obstinacy and a tendency to lonely thought. There are some things which cannot be learned from state documents in record offices; and one of these facts, which is thus apt to escape notice, is how the Narrow Seas impressed their character on these coastal populations. The Narrow Seas are the parents of all the free govern-ments in the world—Holland, England, the United States. The Pilgrim Fathers were their offspring.

The Straits of Dover form the southern apex of the small tri-angle in which the North Sea ends; and they form the north-eastern apex of the triangle where the English Channel narrows down to the twenty miles separating England from the civilized world of Latin influence. On the map it looks the simplest job in the world to sail up the Channel, pass through the Straits, and thence up the estuary of the Thames to London. Alternatively there is the short voyage from Antwerp to London. Philip of Spain saw that. Yet there are only four records of a successful invasion across the Narrow Seas: the Romans, the Saxons, Wil-liam the Conqueror, and the Dutch William the Third. The list suggests high-class efficiency; and it is all wanted for the task. I always suspect that Julius Caesar and his Roman successors had colossal luck in getting across and in getting back. A fog and a gale, with a Roman fleet wrecked on the treacherous sunken sands or blown on to some dangerous headland—Beachy Head, or the South Foreland, or the North Foreland—might have left England barbarous for another four hundred years and have al-tered the history of the world. The chances were heavily against those fair-weather Mediterranean sailors, used to tideless, fogless seas. Perhaps Providence sometimes takes a hand in the game of history.

The Narrow Seas put up almost every form of difficulty known to sailors—tides, fogs, winds, dangerous headlands, sunken shoals. The tides are the foundation of most of the trouble. The North Sea and the Channel act as funnels and concentrate their tides at the Straits. The rise and fall in height is a detail compared to the current, which runs like a race horse. There are four tides a day, two from the north and two from the south. Their relative strengths depend on the winds. Accordingly in the Narrow Seas, four times a day, there is repeated that contest between the North and the South which makes the history of Europe throughout the ages.

These currents have formed shoals which run northward from the Straits of Dover to the mouth of the Thames. My earliest recollections are entwined with flash lights from the lightships on the Goodwin Sands. We could see them on winter evenings from our nursery windows at the top of the house. Sometimes during a fog the boom of a gun would be heard at slow intervals across the sea. It was a ship ashore on the Goodwin Sands. At other times we saw rockets rise mysteriously from the dark waters. It was the Gull lightship signaling a wreck. Next day we were taken down to the harbour, and there was the lifeboat decked with flags: during the night it had been out and had saved the crew of some vessel slowly sinking in the merciless quicksands.

The navigation of the Narrow Seas is the key to Dutch and English history. There are perils in every direction; there are winds and currents to carry you to them; and there are fogs and blinding storms of sleet to hide all knowledge of your where-abouts. The Dutch and English sailors learned their lesson on the the Narrow Seas. The Spanish sailors were used to galleys in the tideless Mediterranean and to huge galleons which ran before the trade winds across the open water of the South Atlantic. When it came to fighting for freedom in the Narrow Seas the oar-driven galleys and the unhandy galleons were helpless. It was no use trusting to oars for large ships in the chops of the Channel: and if you could not sail close to the wind you could say your prayers, for your last moment had come.

As you read a history book, compiled by a learned landsman, it is not so easy to understand why the Armada bolted in terror when it had reached its appointed destination between Antwerp and England. King Philip's strategy must have seemed perfect as he sat in his study in Madrid. Freedom was saved for the world because he had ordered his fleet to halt in a death trap for that type of vessel. Such craft could anchor in the Downs or in Calais Roads, but they could only move thence by running before the gale and making a bolt for it up the North Sea.

In our parish registers for the year 1588, my father's predecessor in the vicarage had written, "Today buried three sailors from the queene's shippes." I read the entry exactly three hundred years afterward, in the same room in which it has been written. Poor nameless men! I wonder whether they ever knew that they had given their lives for the salvation of English freedom.

Every little harbor along that Kentish coast had, and still has, its lifeboat and its luggers, which, by some mysterious art inbred in the population, keep the seas in all weathers—Deal, Ramsgate, Broadstairs, Kingsgate, Margate, all had these lifeboats, and harbors swarming with luggers and fishing smacks.

The fishermen were decidedly "wet" in the technical American sense of that word. I remember one old man who used to row us children out to bathe from his boat. He was a weather-beaten old fellow, and the philosophy of life which he imparted to our eager ears was that "eating is a beastly habit." We all understood, without explanation, that the great-souled way of life was to sustain it on alcoholic beverages—beer for daily life and brandy for festivals. You may criticize the moral code of these men when you have risked your life in saving others as often as had that old lifeboat's man. He shall not remain nameless: his name was Saxby—"Old Saxby" we called him. In his old age, when we were entrusted to him, he got his livelihood by shrimping and by leasing his rowboat. Old Saxby was more remarkable for obstinacy than for lonely thought. But this sole relic of his conversation proves that even he had elaborated his individual outlook on the universe.

The fishing smacks used to trawl in the neighborhood, and also go farther afield into the North Sea to the Dogger Bank. About every third fish in the North Sea ends by being eaten either in England or in Holland. If you drop a ring, either in Boston or in London, your chance of seeing it again is very small. But if you will send it to the English Fishery Board, they will tie it to the tail of a fish and let it loose in the North Sea; and every third time you will get your ring back.

During the Russo-Japanese War, England and Russia nearly went to war over the fishing smacks on the Dogger Bank. The Russian fleet going from the Baltic to Japan, where the Japanese sank it in *their* Narrow Seas, crossed the Dogger Bank in the nighttime and found it studded with small boats and lights. They concluded that they had fallen into an ambush of Japanese torpedo boats, and accordingly opened fire on the fishing smacks. England was aflame with indignation. But luckily Mr. Balfour, the then Prime Minister, and the Lords of the Admiralty—who in England play the august part of your Supreme Court here— kept their heads. The naval officers said that, if you thought you saw a hostile torpedo boat, you had to shoot first and inquire afterward—since there was not time for the converse procedure —and Mr. Balfour remembered that the Russians were probably ignorant of the peculiarities of the Narrow Seas. So the Russian fleet was allowed to pass through the British squadron, and sailed on to its appointed doom.

II

The history of the world depends on a lot of little things, apart from which events would have happened differently. London would never have been heard of as a great centre of commerce unless just to the north of the Straits of Dover there had been a magnificent anchorage off Deal. It is called the Downs. In English naval history the Downs loom large. With an east wind a sailing ship bound from London southward cannot tack and get round the capes of the South Foreland and Beachy Head. The Narrow Seas, at their narrowest part, forbid that. So in old days the ships from London anchored in the Downs. They wanted good anchorage there: on the French side lies Cape Gris-Nez, on the English side there is the South Foreland, and a few miles behind, ready to engulf them lie the Goodwin Sands with the treacherous water rippling over them. It is not healthy to be caught in a gale in that spot without good anchorage. The Downs have lost their importance in these days of steam; but in my boyhood I have seen a hundred sail anchored in the Downs. Such a sight might have been seen for centuries, but now the Downs have disappeared from history.

In 1871, during the Franco-German War, an English squadron anchored in the Downs for months. I remember being taken out to see the battleships. In those days all but one had sails as well as steam power. During the Great War it would have been certain destruction to anchor in the Downs. The haunts of my boyhood in Ramsgate fared badly then: a bomb fell on the house where I was born, another in the garden where I played, and a third blew up a powder magazine on the quay where Old Saxby used to embark us for bathing. I do not think anyone left the town by reason of these little incidents. People repaired their windowpanes and stuck it out with East Kent obstinacy. Certainly my own aunt, who still lives there, never moved her establishment.

But at that game of determination Yorkshire beats us hollow. During the war a general examination of all the school children in Scarborough, a seaside town of Yorkshire, had been arranged by the local authorities to take place from nine to twelve in the morning. At six on that morning three German cruisers appeared and shelled the place for over an hour. It never occurred to the authorities to put off the examination, or to the parents to keep the children from school; nor was the work of the children in any way affected. By the time the examination had begun, a British squadron had turned up, and a North Sea fog had descended to save the Germans; so the townspeople did what they always have done in a fog—they went on with their appointed work.

I wonder if you noticed the names of the little Kentish seaports which I mentioned: Ramsgate, Broadstairs, Kingsgate, and Margate. To a man of Kent—Kentishmen are an inferior brand who live at the west end of the country beyond the River Medway—to a man of Kent these names by their very form all suggest the white chalk cliffs of Old England. These cliffs are perpendicular, with "gaps" or "gates" in them at intervals. Wherever there is a gate there is a small fishing town. I suppose that some early Anglo-Saxon pirate got weary of these endless "gates," and so preferred "stairs" for the Broadstairs "gate."

III

When the Anglo-Saxons grew tired of piracy and took to Christianity and the quiet life, they were bothered by the piratical habits of their unconverted cousins in Scandinavia. So all the old villages and churches are about one to two miles inland. Behind the gaps which lie around the headland of the North Foreland there stands a magnificent group of eleventh-century Norman churches—Minster, St. Laurence behind Ramsgate, St. Peter's behind Broadstairs, St. John's behind Margate, and Monkton. If you do not understand something about life in the eleventh century when you have visited these, you are incapable of learning. They all have one very useful characteristic. They could hold all the villagers of those times; and when the massive oak doors were shut and barred, from the top of the square Kentish flint tower, with the aid of a few arrows and stones, you could watch the pirates till they went off with the next tide.

I do not mean to imply that the inhabitants were foolishly peaceable; because they weren't. Modern America has nothing to teach East Kent in the way of bootlegging. We finally gave it up with the advent of free trade in 1848. But during the Napoleonic Wars the whole population, country gentlemen, magistrates, and clergy, took a hand in the trade. In those good old days the Established Church showed a surprising liberality of sentiment. The services at Minster Church had sometimes to be interrupted to enable the congregation to remove the brandy from the church vaults to neighboring marshes on the rumored approach of the preventive men. In my father's vicarage garden at St. Peter's there were caves with legends of smugglers attached to them.

In recent years the population has been diluted by the influx of Londoners, rich and poor, seeking health from the bracing sea air which comes straight down from the North Pole over the North Sea. But throughout the nineteenth century the East Kent population was devoted to Church and State and moderate Whig principles. My grandfather was a Whig in 1815 when Whiggism was dangerous; he voted Whig in 1832 when Whiggism was all-powerful; and he voted Whig in his old age when Mr. Gladstone triumphed in the early 1870's. Throughout the nineteenth century in East Kent the clergy were the real leaders of the people; bootlegging at the beginning, social reform in the middle—it was all one to them. They were all sturdy Englishmen, clergy and laity together. At the beginning of the century Mr. Harvey, the vicar of St. Laurence, was highly respected, and very deservedly so, though he shared in the jovial habits of that period and sometimes was taken home in a wheelbarrow like Mr. Pickwick. He was a man of energy, and formed the new parish of Ramsgate, which had outgrown its mother village of St. Laurence. His son, Mr. Richard Harvey, was appointed to the new Ramsgate church; and in the second quarter of the century, till 1860, presided there amid universal respect, exhibiting the reformed manners of the new age. In fact he was even High-Church, and introduced an altar cloth with the sacred monogram which can be read at the Latin capital letters IHS. This aroused some Protestant feeling, which was allayed only by the happy conjecture that the letters stood for Jenkins, Harvey, and Snowden—the surnames of the vicar and his two curates. This is an interesting example of how religious strife can be allayed by the ingenuity of scholarship.

The population was very Protestant, but curiously antagonistic to the Nonconformist minority whose theological principles were identical with its own. About 1830 an old gentleman—Townsend was his name—made a vow that if ever he entered a Nonconformist place of worship he hoped that God would make him stick in the doorway. He took the vow seriously, for, when a respected Nonconformist died, during the funeral service he stood outside the church by way of respect, but did not venture into the doorway. In those days there was no honeyed sentiment about the union of the churches.

Throughout the middle of the century the vicar of St. Laurence was Mr. Sicklemore, a considerable landowner who lived in a small park in the parish. He was in the incarnation of "Church and State" sentiment. Even in his own time he represented an England that was fast passing. He had a magnificent voice and always preached in black kid gloves. The sermons expressed his sentiments about things in general, frankly expressed in the vernacular. Here is one of his perorations, which modern America might take to heart:

"This Sunday morning, as I walked through my village, I saw its very walls defaced by advertisements. It's shocking! 'Pon my honor, it's shocking!"

And with that beautiful sentiment he dismissed the congregation. I can well remember Mr. Sicklemore; and I cannot begin to imagine his sentiments if some enterprising medium should evoke him to a knowledge of the modern world.

I think my father was the last example of these East Kent clergymen who were really homogeneous with their people, and therefore natural leaders on all occasions, secular and religious. The present-day English clergy are excellent men, but they are divorced from the soil. My father could remember the arrival of the first railway engine in Ramsgate, and he died at the end of the century. So he exactly represents the period of transformation. He had all the habits of thought of a man who had always taken the lead, not because he thought about it, but because it was the natural thing to do. He was entirely devoid of any artificial tone of "uplift." In fact he hated it, and expressed his opinion of "cant" with direct Saxon vigor. But in his generation a tenderness of tone had crept in, and he was an example of it. When the Baptist minister of the village was dying, my father was the only minister whom he would see. Despite all the differences between their churches they were both East Kent men; and when they read the Bible together they understood each other without many words.

In his youth he had ridden with the hounds, and had a magnificent seat on horseback. He had also played cricket with every club in the neighborhood. He knew all the farmers and the laborers; and in his later years he had christened a fair percentage of them, after playing cricket or hunting with their fathers in earlier days when they were boys together.

He was an equal mixture of a High-Churchman and a Broad-Churchman. His favourite history was Gibbon's *Decline and Fall.* I do not think that any of Gibbon's chapters shocked him; for his robust common sense told him that the people of East Kent, with whom he was quite content, were really very unlike the early Christians. His favorite character in the Bible was Abraham, who exhibits many features to endear him to the East Kent mentality.

My father was a natural orator, equally at home in the pulpit or at a mass meeting either of townspeople or of countrymen. His church was always crammed with the villagers, and with townspeople who had walked some miles, and with Londoners spending their holidays in the district.

These East Kent clergy of the old school had a simpler view of the relations of a pastor to his flock than that which prevails at present. They viewed with disapproval the growth of the complex parochial machinery which obtains at present throughout England. It was a case of one-man rule. They were simple and direct in their methods, and yet they got at the heart of the people in a way denied to the present generation. As they walked through their villages, or across the country footpaths, they stopped and chatted with every man, woman, or child whom they met. They knew all about them—whether their patch of vegetable garden was good or bad, whether they were sober or whether they drank, what their fathers were like, and how their sons had turned out. They had homely advice and kindly sympathy to give. Above all, they saw to it that every child in the village went to school and had an education according to the lights of those days. They visited the schools, listened to the children, patted them on the head, and made friends with the school-teachers. It was a humanizing, kindly influence, which trusted mainly to the mercy of God to save the souls of men.

IV

This corner of Kent is called the Isle of Thanet. The arm of the sea which separates it from the mainland had just ceased to be navigable when the Tudors came to the throne. Now its old bed forms desolate grass flats surrounded by tidal ditches. This flat marshy country is from four to six miles broad and about twenty miles long. It is protected from the North Sea by a dike in the Dutch fashion. The connection with the Low Countries used to be closer than it is now. England supplied the raw materials for the industrial cities, such as Ghent and Bruges. The sixteenth- and seventeenth-century cottages are all identical with the corresponding cottages in Flanders. Sandwich, once the chief naval dockyard of England, is an old Dutch town, so far as its buildings are concerned. Its importance finally ceased in the seventeenth century when its harbor silted up in consequence of the closing of the sea channel between Thanet and the mainland. If you go there, you will find quiet Dutch streets, a glorious Norman church, and in the old Townhall contemporary pictures of the sea fights with the Dutch. In the intervals of fighting their Protestant kinsfolk for the sake of trade, they got over some Flemish men "cunning in waterworks," as their records say. But even these engineers were powerless against the tides of the Narrow Seas, which remorselessly rolled up sand till Sandwich joined with Ravenna in Italy to exemplify how puny are the efforts of man to stay the hand of Fate.

The witness of Sandwich, the lonely marsh telling of the lost sea passage, and the wonderful group of Norman churches, and in the far distance to the west the towers of Canterbury Cathedral, all proclaim that we are in the midst of a district where events have happened which shaped England. It is natural that it should be so, for we are at the very focus of the Narrow Seas.

Place yourself at the southwest angle of the finest of all these Norman churches, the church of Minster in Thanet, now some four miles from the apex of a large shallow bay dividing the two capes, the North Foreland, in Thanet, and the South Foreland, near Dover on the mainland in Kent. Parts of the church are older than the Normans: the small tower behind us is mainly Saxon, but some of its masonry is Roman. Inside the church there is an oak chest said to have been brought over with William the Conqueror—the heavy luggage of some Norman knight. This is the spot which best overlooks what in old times was the main gateway into England from the French coast. The marshes at our feet stretch up to Canterbury to the west; on the south their seashore looks toward France; and on the north another shore touches the estuary of the Thames. Till near the end of the Middle Ages these marshes formed the sea passage; and the traffic to London passed through it, avoiding the dangerous voyage round the North Foreland.

Roman soldiers guarded forts, Richborough and Reculver—Rutupiae and Regulbium—which still exist at either end of it. Reculver retains only the foundations, with twin mediaeval towers to mark the desolateness of its present site. Richborough still shows the massive Roman walls round the huge enclosure. Then Thanet was an island, and Minster in Thanet overlooked the seaway near the Richborough end. From that position you can see the spot where Hengist and Horsa landed with the first band of Saxons, and also, one hundred and fifty years later, Saint Augustine—the missionary, not the theologian. The first Saxons and the first Christian missionaries landed in Thanet for the same reason, because both they and the inhabitants of Kent felt safer with an arm of the sea between them.

Till the beginning of the nineteenth century an old oak tree could be pointed out near the church, under which Augustine is said to have first preached Christianity to Ethelbert, the king of Kent. All the sermons to be delivered in New England next Sunday morning are derived from that ancestor which still haunts the sea winds in the churchyard of Minster in Thanet.

Ethelbert died at Reculver more than thirteen hundred years ago, and its modern desolateness seems to stand guardian over those simple remote times when the pagan king became Christian. Across the marshes you can on a clear day see the towers of Canterbury Cathedral. In St. Martin's Church, just above the Cathedral, is the font in which Ethelbert was baptized. Even in Ethelbert's time the building was a restoration; it was an old Roman church put in order for his Christian wife. In the Cathedral you are shown the stone in the pavement on which Becket fell as he was murdered by Reginald Fitzurse and his companion knights who with him had hurried across the Narrow Seas from France. "The traitor will never rise again!" cried his murderers.

It was a false boast, often repeated on like occasions. Becket is one of the greatest of those traitors who have "risen again" in English history as immortal patriots, glorious for resistance to brute force by whomsoever wielded, King, Parliament, or People. Opposite to this spot, on the other side of the Cathedral, the armor of the Black Prince hangs, reminiscent of the battle of Crecy. In the Cathedral there is a Brenchley chapel. The modern Brenchleys were agricultural laborers in my father's parish, thus exemplifying the rule that the descendants of the mediaeval barons are chiefly to be found among the peasantry.

Finally, coming back to modern times and to our observation post in the Minster churchyard, we could see thence, during the Great War, train after train of ammunition, in endless procession, pass along the little branch railway track which runs through the marshes from Canterbury to Minster, and thence past Richborough to Sandwich. Richborough had awakened from the sleep of centuries. At its feet the mouth of a small stream forms a harborage in the marsh, guarded from the air by the mist which for a thousand years had arisen each night finally to perform this last service to freedom, and protected from the sea by a devious passage amid sand banks. In my childhood I have watched a horse sucked down into the quicksands of that bay, the rider barely escaping. This spot again became a gateway from England to France. The English ammunition was transported across the Narrow Seas in barges or on train ferries. A battleship was moored with its guns trained on the bay across which the Romans, the Saxons, and Augustine had sailed.

Once more the scene has relapsed into its age-long quiet; and yet, as you stand and absorb it into your being, it takes its character from haunting memories, and from the solitary cry of a sea gull sounding like a stray echo from the past.

The small tower of Roman and Saxon masonry in the church-yard of Minster in Thanet, facing the Narrow Seas where the North Sea meets the English Channel, and Plymouth Rock, sheltered by Cape Cod from the Atlantic Ocean, are the two spots which mark the two origins—the English origin and the American origin, separated by a thousand years—of a new type of civilized culture, now becoming dominant wherever lands of temperate climate border upon seas and oceans.

V

An Appeal to Sanity

_____

IN international relations the world alternates between contrasting phases, resulting from variation of emotion between the phases of low and high tension.

In the low phase, a disturbance in one region due to some specific disorder remains local. It does not arouse emotions elsewhere. In such circumstances international relations take the form of local agreements or of local disputes, sometimes culminating in local wars. Determinate finite questions are in this way settled one by one, without reference to each other.

In the phase of high tension, vivid emotions excite each other, and tend to spread throughout the nations, disturbing every variety of topic.

To-day the world is plunged in this second phase of contagious emotion. Thus, in the survey which constitutes this appeal, no item can be considered separately.

What is the justification of "isolation" on the part of a powerful nation, when evil is turbulent in any part of the world?

The answer is that history discloses habitual disorganization among nations, somewhere or other. War is a throwback from civilization for victors and vanquished, whatever be the initial objects of these crusades. Even presupposing victory, we must weigh carefully the losses against the gains.

Thus the habitual policy should be "Isolation—Unless . . ."

Each nation is a trustee for the fostering of certain types of civilization within areas for which it is directly responsible. Its supreme duty is there. Thus a nation should remain isolated, *unless* (1) the evils of the world threaten this supreme duty, or (2) these evils can be rectified by an effort which will not indirectly defeat the performance of this special duty.

I

Now as to England. This country is a European island with a world-wide coordinating influence of many types. The continental civilization of Europe, and its political organizations, develop with singularly little reference to England. Throughout the last four hundred years the keynote of the English policy in Europe has been *safety,* and otherwise *isolation* (nonintervention)—that is, such isolation as is consistent with safety. The result has been that English policy is mainly directed to the western fringe of Europe. Regarding the interior of Europe the interest of England is indirect, and has been so from the Tudor times onward.

To justify this attitude we must refer to the English "world-wide coordinating influence," for which the popular designation is the ambiguous term "Empire."

In Burma and India there are almost 400,000,000 people, sensitive, acute, backward in modern techniques, with innumerable diversities. This population is nearly three times that of the United States. It requires, above all, coordination of its ancient civilizations with modern techniques. It requires generations of peace. For England, Central Europe is a remote detail compared to this problem—that is to say, it is a detail if, as Englishmen, we consider our supreme duty. Our Empire isolates us from Europe—safety excepted.

Then there is the Mahometan world, beyond the Empire, but influencing and influenced. It lies around the route to India and within India. It spreads over North Africa, interwoven with English interests in Egypt, the Sudan, and Upper Nigeria. It touches the Atlantic Ocean.

Finally there are the self-governing Dominions, and other districts only partially autonomous. This confederation requires quiet growth. In varying degrees it is sensitive to the disorders of the world.

Thus English policy should be basically non-European. In England excited intellectuals are focused upon Europe. The mass of the population remembers its intimate relationships across the oceans—parents, children, cousins.

To understand English policy and its vacillations one must realize that intellectuals of every social grade are interested in the old European civilization, and that the masses gaze beyond the oceans. In Cornwall you will find in most cottages pictures of mining districts throughout the world; in Cambridgeshire I have presided over a village meeting aroused to a storm of indignation over some army regulation about service abroad. Our best garden boy emigrated to Canada. In Wiltshire there lived near our summer cottage an old man who had been in India, serving in the ranks. Such people have no direct connection with Central Europe. English policy sways between these two foci of interest, and has done so for centuries: Europe and the world.

In the confused sociological topics which constitute international relations, there are no clear issues. Such premises are either before their times or behind their times, and only rarely with their times. Sometimes they have no contact with temporal events. They are useful as suggestions to enlighten the imagination in its dealings with practical affairs.

English foreign interests at the present moment can be vaguely classified under four headings, so far as immediate dangers are concerned—Central Europe, the Mediterranean, the Jews, and the Mahometans.

Central Europe, in its form up to the year 1938, had its origin in the Versailles Treaty and the League of Nations. Both these fundamental elements—the Treaty and the League—have suffered incessant violations and repudiations by every group of every opinion. In the negotiations which framed the Treaty, and in the subsequent repudiation of the sanctity of the Treaty, America took the lead—perhaps rightly. Thus even the vague sanctity of international law ceases to apply either to the Treaty or to the League. At the present moment they are historical reminiscences. They impose the minimum of obligation. Obligation, in European foreign policy, arises from the facts of the immediate situation and from duty to the future. Formal law can refer only to situations sufficiently stable.

The main motives generating excitement in Central Europe are (1) nationality, based upon various modes of community— such as language, analogies of physiological character, contiguity; (2) doctrines of social organization—liberal, dictatorial, communistic, capitalistic, religious; (3) economic opportunity. None of these motives is completely evil or completely good. Their moral justification depends on the particular circumstances of each case.

The social system of Central Europe is very unstable from the Baltic to the Black Sea, and throughout the Balkan States. There is no complete solution. We can only hope for something that survives with the minimum suppression of dominant aspirations. The point to notice is that war, even if successful, can only increase the malignant excitement. The remedy is peace, fostering the slow growth of civilized feelings. War may be necessary to guard world civilization. But for Central Europe the effective remedy is *peace.*

In Central Europe, the immediate focus of interest has been Czechoslovakia. This is a composite state created by the Treaty of Versailles. All states are composite in origin. The essential question is the mutual agreement of the various factors. The name "Czechoslovakia" tells only half the tale. The full name should be Czecho-Slovak-Magyar-Ruthenian-Polish-Germania.

Having regard to genius, moral heroism, and tormented suffering, the histories of Czechs, Magyars, and Poles present three poignant tragedies which together constitute the tragedy of Central Europe. From century to century, from generation to generation, uncertain boundaries sway to and fro. By choosing your date you can make any claim for any one of them. Each group was surrounded by populations repugnant to itself—for some reason of religion or habit of life. Bohemia, Poland, Hungary, each in its own way tells a tale of the horror of history, and of the genius of mankind. In other words, *tragedy.*

The Great War immensely strengthened feelings of national unity and desires for national independence. The historical reasons for these feelings in different national groups are not to the point. The essential fact is their existence today. As peace approached, President Wilson proclaimed the satisfaction of these aspirations after national consolidation as one of the aims of the war. This objective was unanimously accepted by all concerned.

This clarity was deceptive. The Czech State could be made

adequately self-sufficient only by including alien groups, for economic reasons and for purposes of defense. Also within it, as in other states, populations were intermixed. Thus, swayed by a legitimate admiration of the Czechs and by hopes for acquiescence in unification, the treaty makers provided the Czech State with an amplitude of extension over a fringe of diverse groups. There was nothing necessarily wrong in this policy. It might have succeeded, in another century, or in the absence of German, Magyar, and Polish states across the border. The plain essential fact remains that the experiment has not succeeded now. Also the revolt can appeal to the great principle of nationality, proclaimed by President Wilson, and in 1918 accepted by the whole world.

Is a world war to be waged in support of the thesis that this great doctrine does not apply to Germans, or to Poles, or to Hungarians? At the time of the Versailles settlement some members of the Labor Party in England protested against the inclusions of alien populations in the Bohemian State. After twenty years some of their successors are prepared to fight for its maintenance. Up to a few months ago, the very mention of military armament provoked horrified resistance from the same party. Today they clamor for a crusade in Central Europe, depending for success on the intervention of the Heavenly Powers. It is one lesson of history that these last-mentioned powers are usually on the side of common sense. Of course, miracles do happen; but it is unwise to expect them.

II

Since the World War the recovery of Germany has mainly taken the form of consolidating the Germans of Europe into a unified German State. This process has been in accordance with the dominant feelings of the populations concerned. Also these feelings are grounded in a long historical tradition. Between Waterloo and the Austro-Prussian war of 1866 there existed a loose confederation with Austria and Prussia as its leading members. From the time of Charlemagne to that of the French Revolution, a period of almost a thousand years, each century produced some form of Germanic unity, more or less. This wavering exhibition of unity is termed, in history, the Holy Roman Empire. Thus the present unification of Germans into Germany is grounded on traditions of feelings which survive the oscillations of history. It is a sensible policy to respect it. To have a world war in opposition to this Pan-German movement would be madness. The United States would be the first power to adopt an unfriendly neutrality, when the mass of its population had been aroused to survey the situation. Its widespread attitude of criticism of its allies in the last war teaches a lesson which is not ignored by European statesmen.

Other nations, whose attitude is relevant to success, would be even more unfriendly. In fighting to maintain frontiers of the Czech State, we should be thwarting the keenest aspirations of the Poles and Hungarians. Thus we should have against us three great examples in Europe of thwarted aspiration after national unity. And what would be our justification? The sanctity of the Treaty of Versailles, and the fact that the Czechs would be more prosperous if their pre-existing frontiers were retained. Expansion for the sake of prosperity can be justified only by the reciprocal acquiescence and prosperity of the populations thus included. War on behalf of the frontiers of Czechoslovakia as determined by the Treaty of Versailles would have the weakest moral justification, and would involve active or passive opposition from states whose support is essential for success.

Is Germany to be allowed to extend her direct power over the whole of Central and Western Europe? The answer is that Germany (or any state) should be forcibly prevented when three conditions are fulfilled:—

(1) When she is violently interfering with the development of other states, without the justification of establishing any principle of social coordination, acknowledged as of prime importance;

(2) When the consequences of an attempt at forcible prevention will not be worse than the consequences of acquiescence;

(3) When such an attempt can secure its direct object.

In all human affairs abstract notions apply vaguely—more or less; we must be content with approximation. Also reasons merge into each other. For example, these three conditions overlap, and have no sharp distinction. But they do represent large approximations, which sometimes are adequate justifications for action, either separately or jointly.

It has been argued that condition No. 1 is not satisfied in respect to the Czechslovakian question. But this conclusion bears upon the status of condition No. 2. For, owing to the fact that Poland and Hungary feel the same grievance—namely, that their minorities were included in the Czech State—it follows that a war waged by Britain and France on behalf of the Czechs would have involved Poland and Hungary in unfriendly neutrality, if not in active opposition. The two great Western democracies could not have chosen a worse test case.

Further, neither France nor Great Britain can directly reach the Czech State, to secure its immediate defense. Also, their war preparations still suffer from reliance on a League of Nations with mythical omnipotence. Thus victory could be achieved only by a long-drawn-out war of attrition. The populations of Europe would suffer years of acute misery. Millions of human beings would be killed. The young, active, and enterprising part of the population would supply most of the casualties. Europe would emerge exhausted, with its emotions barbarized, its ideals brutalized. Also, Czechoslovakia would have vanished.

In the preceding argument two factors have been omitted: (1) an estimate of Hitler's action in the face of threats; and (2) Russia in the background. Would Hitler have given way if England and France had threatened war? Hitler bears no analogy to the kings, presidents, and prime ministers who achieve their positions by the normal working of established constitutions. Such people can retreat or resign. They retain a great position and high respect. Such men can estimate the consequences of the future with emotions guided by reason as it surveys situations settled as to their general structure.

For rulers such as Hitler and Mussolini the emotional situation is entirely altered. Their own safety and that of their cause depend upon an atmosphere of inflamed emotion. In this way their power arose; in this way it maintains itself. The alternative for them is a dungeon and a firing squad. Hitler is an enraged mystic; that is to say, he belongs to one species of prophet. He is not primarily thinking of personal safety. He is enjoying the hysteria which is the very life-blood of his cause. What is the sense of saying that such a man in such circumstances, knowing the strength of his opportunity with Poland and Hungary wavering, with his armies and air force ready, with his knowledge of the temporary weakness of England owing to the block to armament persistently maintained by idealists out of touch with reality—what is the sense of believing that Hitler, with these emotions and with this opportunity, would allow himself to be bluffed into inaction? It might have happened so, because miracles are always possible.

But, ought this miracle to happen? We have already seen that, for the settlement of Central Europe, the release of the alien populations of Bohemia from inclusion in its state was the very solution advocated by these idealists at the time of the Versailles Treaty. It is the readjustment most likely to appease Europe. If our policy is the appeasement of inflamed emotions by the removal of causes of irritation, this should be our first step. It is unfortunate that the present crisis was required to bring it about. Such is history in all ages.

How is the preceding argument affected by the existence of Russia?

Russia is more than the eastern fringe of Central Europe and the northwestern fringe of China, with armed forces capable of producing predetermined results beyond these borders. We have omitted the one of most decisive importance for the future of the world—namely, the southeastern boundary, which touches the whole length of the central portion of the Mahometan world.

But Russia is more than its boundaries, just as America is more than its Atlantic and Pacific seaboards. The Encyclopoedia states, "[Russia] is thus the largest unbroken political unit in the world and occupies more than one seventh of the land surface of the globe." What is happening within this great territory? At times we learn of the execution of a batch of generals, or of a batch of political officers, or of a batch of industrial technicians. But we hardly know the reasons. We know little of the mental and physical health of the men in command. We know nothing of the emotions seething throughout the vast stretch of its population. Has the ideal of national coordination superseded the initial ideal of international revolution? We do not know. We gain little from the reports of men, however able and disinterested, who have lived for a few years in Moscow. There are three thousand miles from the Ural Mountains to Vladivostok, and a thousand miles from the Polish border to the Ural Mountains. It is difficult to fathom the emotional reactions of a hundred and fifty million people scattered over this vast region.

The country has just passed through the greatest sudden revolution in history. A moronic dynasty and an upper class, brilliant in all respects with the single exception of its complete political failure, have been exterminated. The revolution was horrible, but probably beneficial.

One fact seems as well established as any other, in the doubtful maze of Russian policy: namely, Russian statesmen of all parties have a contempt for the liberal democratic type of state, illustrated by America, France, England, Scandinavia, Holland. They have no use for that mode of organization. Suppose that war had been declared, and that the Russian armies had successfully established themselves in Central Europe, with Bohemia as their base. Russian statesmanship would have been all-powerful in that region. Neither England nor France could send a soldier there. Is it sensible to assume that Russian statesmanship would be satisfied to have secured the nice little Czech State on the liberal lines approved by America? Surely we can wipe that dream out of the picture. Poland, Rumania, Hungary, and Yugoslavia would have been in a turmoil, the ultimate issue completely uncertain. Tens of millions would have died. The Russian state organization may be better than the present German state system, but the issue of a Central European war, with Russia involved, may produce any mode of social settlement devised in Heaven or in Hell, or by the usual collaboration of both. The only certainty would be a ghastly slaughter leading to an unknown future. The whole drama would be very exciting for idealists watching from the safety of distance. The great probability is that initially the Russian war machine would be very ineffective. There would be a long war.

Yet again essential factors in this crisis of world history have been omitted—the Mahometan world, Italy, the Jews.

If war by ill chance should break out now, there seems little doubt that Italy will join Germany. The effect of this alliance immensely strengthens the preceding arguments. France will be hampered on another frontier. The French fleet and part of the English fleet will be tied in the Mediterranean. Our pressure on Germany in the North Sea and the Baltic will be to that extent diminished. The war will be longer and more destructive. Eighty-five million people in Great Britain and France will be facing a hundred and twenty million in Germany and Italy. It will be a long pull. The issue of wars does not wholly depend on the count of populations. Also there is the good hope that Russia would intervene and redress this balance.

But at what a cost! Years of war in Central Europe, and the whole Mediteranean world a turmoil of disorder.

We must now consider the Mahometan world. Recent discussions on international relations seem to have been conducted by one-eyed men. There is a renaissance in progress stretching throughout the great region of the ancient and mediaeval civilizations from Persia to Mesopotamia, throughout Asia Minor, Syria, and Arabia, and reaching to Egypt. In these regions civilization was born, and in various transformations it flourished till it was overwhelmed in mediaeval times by hordes from Central Asia. The old populations remain, and to-day there is recovery. Persian, Turkish, and the various Arabian nations have able and sensible rulers. Egypt is well governed. But the populations are as yet naive politically, liable to spasmodic outbreaks.

In case of war, with Italy, Russia, France, England involved, there can be little doubt that the whole of this central region of the Mahometan faith will be reduced to turmoil. Peace is required. There are two hundred million Mahometans in the world. Are their interests to be neglected in comparison with the importance of retaining four million Germans, Poles, and Hungarians, against their will, as subjects of the Bohemian State?

III

To-day the most universal problem is the relation of the Jews to the various countries in which they dwell. Our modern progressive civilization owes its origin mainly to the Greeks and the Jews. The progressiveness is the point to be emphasized. China and India long ago attained to types of life with more delicate aesthetic and philosophic appreciations, in some respects, than our Western type. But they reached a level and stayed there. The Greeks and the Jews, in the few centuries before and after the beginning of the Christian Era, intensified an element of progressive activity which was diffused throughout the many peoples in the broad belt from Mesopotamia to Spain. Political stability is not the point. We are considering ideals shaping emotions and thus issuing into conduct. This progressive character must be kept in mind. So far as Greeks and Jews were active, progress was not in a rut, degenerating into conservation.

The Roman Empire was a great creation. But no Roman ever disclosed a new idea in religion, in science, in philosophy, in art, in literature, or even in the law which is called Roman. The sustained habit of progressive activity was the discovery of Greeks and Semites in the marvelous thousand years which precede and include the foundation of Christianity.

The Greeks have vanished. The Jews remain.

The Jews are unpopular in many lands. In this fact there is nothing to arouse surprise. In England, with its tendency to relapse into a rut of tradition, the Scotch people were unpopular throughout the eighteenth century, after their union with England in the year 1707. They were performing for England services analogous to those of the Jews for all the races west of India and Central Asia. English literature in the eighteenth century, so far as thought is concerned, would be in a poor way if Scotch and Irish contributions were withdrawn. What brilliance was contributed to English politics throughout the nineteenth century by Gladstone the Scot, and Disraeli the Jew! They transgressed the average limitations. Apart from ability, differences are quite enough to create prejudices.

Thus, in approaching the Jewish problem as it exists to-day, we are considering one of the factors operative to sustain the many values of life. The question at issue is not the happiness of a finite group. It is the fate of our civilization.

To-day civilization is in danger by reason of a perversion of doctrine concerning the social character of humanity. The worth of any social system depends on the value experience it promotes among individual human beings. There is no one American value experience other than the many experiences of individual human beings. There is no one American value experience other than the many experiences of individual Americans or of other individuals affected by American life. A community life is a mode of eliciting value for the people concerned.

It is true that there is a mystic sense of the coordination and eternity of realized value. But we here approach the basic doctrine of religion. To attach that coordination of value to a finite social group is a lapse into barbaric polytheism.

Further, each human being is a more complex structure than

any social system to which he belongs. Any particular community life touches only part of the nature of each civilized man. If the man be wholly subordinated to the common life, he is dwarfed. His complete nature lies idle, and withers. Communities lack the intricacies of human nature. The beauty of a family is derivative from its members. The family life provides the opportunity; the realization lies in the individuals.

Thus social life is the provision of opportunity. If that opportunity be conceived as complete subordination to the limitations of one community, human nature is dwarfed. Render unto Caesar the things that are Caesar's. But beyond Caesar there stretches the array of aspirations whose coordinating principle is termed God. It is not to be found in any one simple community life, either economic or knit by aim at domination. Even a religious community is inadequate. There always remains *solus cum solo.* We have developed a moral individuality; and in that respect we face the universe—*alone.*

This is the justification of that liberalism, that zeal for freedom, which underlies the American Constitution and other various forms of democratic government.

It is the reason why the "totalitarian" doctrine is hateful. Governments are clumsy things, inadequate to their duties. A wise government makes provision for the interweaving of alternative forms of community life. The most valuable part of legal doctrine is concerned with the relation of the state to this indefinite group of communities within, and around, it. In this way an international element becomes an essential factor in human life.

Today, by the introduction of modern techniques, the interrelations of human beings throughout this planet have reached an intimate importance far beyond anything dreamt of in past ages, even in the early lifetime of older people now living. Science is international and requires international relations among its societies. Art, literature, religion, and commerce are international.

In the simple age of mediaeval Europe, the clergy and the Jews served the main purposes of interweaving the varieties of life into a unity of progress. And the clergy were the representatives of the interaction of Greek and Jewish mentalities in previous centuries.

For two and a half thousand years, Semites have continuously provided suggestion, novelty, and achievement, whereby the life of Europe never lost the subconscious ideal of progress.

Of course the Jews are not the only factor producing progress in Western life. But their services have been immense. Also, in the long run, no written document or artistic structure can perform this service. For example, it is possible, and almost usual, to construe the Bible, Greek literature, and the American Constitution with all the limitations of their periods of origin. And then these heritages from the past are transformed into barriers to progress instead of its foundation. In asserting this danger, I am merely repeating the Catholic doctrine that a living Church is required to interpret lifeless documents. Many living agencies are required to transform our experience of the world that has been into our ideal of the world that shall be.

It is for this reason that the Jews have been a priceless factor in the advance of European civilization. They belong to each nation, and yet they import a tinge of internationalism. They are eager in respect to concepts relevant to progress, just where we have forgotten them. They have a slight—ever so slight—difference of reaction to those commandments which disclose ideals of perfection. They constitute one of those factors from which each period of history derives its originality.

To-day we are witnessing a relapse into barbarism. The tendency touches every country. But it is centred in Europe. And in Europe Germany is the main seat of the vicious explosion. The general character is overemphasis on the notion of nationality, producing the ideal of the totalitarian state. The activity, derivative from this debased notion, is the determination to exterminate international factors which exhibit human nature as greater than any state-system. The Jews are the first example of this refusal to worship the state. But religions, arts, and sciences will come next, until mankind are reduced to mean little creatures subservient to the god-state, embodied in some god-man. The worth of life is at stake.

Two problems of pressing importance are made urgent by the anti-Jewish explosion in Germany. How can the Jews in Germany be saved? How can the Jews from Germany and elsewhere be redistributed throughout the world?

It should be realized at once that war is no solution for either of these perplexing duties. An immediate war would probably lead to the massacre of hundreds of thousands of Jews, together with the slaughter of other millions throughout various nations. Europe may be forced into war by the wild lusts of dictatorial states to achieve domination. It is necessary for the democracies to be armed and watchful. But war cannot solve the Jewish question. However successful the crusade, it will leave eighty million Germans with emotions yet more remote from civilized standards.

It is obvious, therefore, that our first task is to undertake the expense of receiving the Jews, and of enabling them to settle elsewhere after such training as is necessary for their new life.

The final problem is the permanent settlement. There is not one solution. There must be many settlements in diverse regions.

In considering such districts we must be careful to judge them in reference to the techniques of the present and the future, and to free our imaginations of pictures derived from a vanished past. This caution especially applies to the large stretch down the East Coast of Africa. Hitherto it has been out of the way and remote. But to-morrow, when airplane traffic has developed, the whole coast line will be intimately connected with Egypt, Palestine, and India. The world is on the eve of a development as important and as revolutionary as that produced by the introduction of railways. Disastrous oversights will be committed by people whose imaginations are fettered to past history.

And yet, in other ways, the converse error of neglecting the lesson of history shows ominous signs of hindering the process of settlement.

The later centuries of Turkish domination in the Mahometan world have been a period of decay in civilization, even before the military power began to ebb. It is doubtful whether the capture of Constantinople was not a greater disaster to Mahometans than to Christians. Probably not, because the Muslim world for three centuries merely shared the common fate of Asia when it came into contact with the progressive techniques of Europe.

Today the tide has turned. Throughout Asia there is a revival. The lesson is being learned. Eastern Asia—namely, China and Japan—is not relevant to this immediate discussion. Consider Southern Asia from Burma and the Malay Peninsula, across India, upward to Persia, across Asia Minor, Syria, and Arabia, across Egypt, across North Africa, and ending at Gibraltar and Nigeria on the shores of the Atlantic. Consider the populations and their cultural influences and the vast stretch of the surface of the world.

Throughout this region, England, France, and Italy exercise

various types of influence. English influence is the most extensive, especially in the numerical count of population. So far as
indigenous military force is concerned, the Mahometan world
is easily the most widespread and important. Also the Mahometan nations are producing vigorous and able rulers, and the Turks
have had one recent genius in Kemal Ataturk.

How is this British imperial influence to be characterized? It
varies from district to district, and from continent to continent.
It touches the two extremes from direct military rule in a few
fortresses to mere diplomatic friendliness, especially with Mahometan nations. The chief feature is the general absence of direct military compulsion, except so far as it is supplied by the
active assistance and the passive support of the populations directly concerned. Throughout the whole of this vast region, with
its thousands of miles of territories and its hundreds of millions
of inhabitants, the number of British soldiers can hardly exceed
one hundred thousand men. Also in Great Britain there is no
large reserve of soldiers, only a few tens of thousands. These
sparse reserves can be quickly transferred to a few spots by transport across the seas. The British Empire in Asia and parts of
North Africa is now a coordinating agency, actively supported
or passively accepted by the populations concerned. It is performing a service, sometimes well, sometimes in mediocre fashion, sometimes very poorly.

How in past times that Empire arose is not to the point. To-
day it is introducing throughout its vast populations those sociological habits and those various coordinations which will enable
them to resume their ancient functions in the advance of civilization.

This Empire is of enormous advantage to Great Britain, chiefly
in two ways. In the first place, it promotes British trade in those

regions; in fact, the Empire arose from that activity. In the second place, it provides civilian employment for a large proportion of the educated classes. Almost every such family has members spread throughout this area. The very army officers turn into governmental agents, governmental advisers, governmental administrators.

The final ideal is a large friendly cooperation of the populations concerned, each self-governing. This ideal is already realized by the confederation of British Dominions. It is an ideal of gradual growth; only within this century has it dominated British policy.

IV

Finally, the Hebrew National Settlement in Palestine remains for examination. Religion has been and is now the major source of those ideals which add to life a sense of purpose that is worthwhile. Apart from religion, expressed in ways generally intelligible, populations sink into the apathetic task of daily survival, with minor alleviations. Throughout the whole continental region under consideration, Palestine is the ideal centre to which various religious faiths converge.

It was the genius of the Jews, their vividness of grasp of the religious problem, which bestowed on Palestine this commanding position. The three Western faiths, Judaism, Christianity, Mahometanism, point thither. The final dispersal of the Jews took place in A.D. 70, when Romans captured Jerusalem. Thus the Jews as a dominating element in the population have been absent for as long a time as they ever occupied the country. It was the Jewish genius that bestowed its radiance upon Palestine. Eighteen hundred years ago!

Thus many claims converge on Palestine—the Jewish claim

in virtue of bygone occupation and of living genius, the Mahometan claim in virtue of age-long occupation and vivid association, and the Christian claim. It must also be remembered that at the end of the Great War the British would not have been in command of Palestine except for the Arab revolt against Turkey, with Lawrence of Arabia coordinating the Arab princes. Concurrently with this revolt, there is the Balfour Declaration, promising British assistance in the establishment of a National Jewish Home in Palestine, in a manner consistent with the rights of the existing Arab population. The carrying out of the policy presents a complex problem; but the policy in itself expresses the complexity of the keen interests which converge upon Palestine, claiming recognition. The whole question was referred to the Arab chieftains, and at the Peace Conference obtained their passive acquiescence. It must also be noted that the Arab princes of the surrounding states, and the Egyptian and Turkish governments, have been conspicuously careful in refraining from intrusion.

The records of the Middle Ages, during the brilliant period of Mahometan ascendancy, afford evidence of joint association of Mahometan and Jewish activity in the promotion of civilization. The culmination of the Middle Ages even in Christian lands was largely dependent upon this association. Thomas Aquinas received Aristotle from it; Roger Bacon received the foundations of modern science from it. The commercial system of the Italian seaports was a copy of the activities throughout the preceding Dark Ages, carried on by Syrians and Jews.

The association of Jews with the Mahometan world is one of the great facts of history from which modern civilization is derived. The Jewish settlement in Palestine has been established with success, in respect to its immediate aims. It has been supported with ability and self-sacrifice. The result has made it evident that the country is capable of supporting yet larger numbers.

There is one exception to this satisfactory issue of the experiment. The Arabs in Palestine are dissatisfied—not all the Arabs, but large sections who are in open revolt. This serious state of things is probably in part due to lack of statesmanlike-initiative on the part of British officials. Some genius was required and failed to appear; perhaps there was positive inefficiency. The situation has not been rescued by them, nor has it been improved by two committees of inquiry dispatched from England.

There is, however, another side to this question, which may produce disaster. Any fusion of Jewish and Arab interests must be produced by the Jews and Arabs themselves. This primary objective of statesmanship seems to have been largely overlooked by the Jewish controlling agencies. It would not be fair to the mass of emigrants from Central Europe to expect from them any insight into the complications of Syrian life; but the controlling agencies in England and the United States might have been asked to show some grasp of the essential objectives.

Unfortunately in public utterances, whatever may have been done behind the scenes, there has predominated the demand that Great Britain should force upon Palestine an unrestricted Jewish domination. In one instance there was even a suggestion that the Jewish agencies should refuse to attend any conference to which dissentient Arabs were to be admitted.

This attitude, if maintained, is signing the death warrant of the Jewish Home in Palestine—perhaps not to-day, but in the near future. In the region of large political affairs, the test of success is twofold—namely, survival power and compromise.

The literary interest of historians is captured by transitory brilliance. Survival power is the basic factor for political success.

For Palestine any immediate solution which depends on the persistent military might of Great Britain is bound to fail. Within the next century there is every prospect that in times of crisis England will be unable to transport sufficient troops. She cannot be depended on to exercise continuous military domination along the Syrian coast. She may return; but continuity is unlikely.

Any convulsion within the vast area of British influence may occupy her reserves of military strength, which merely amount to an adequate police force. When this happens, a convulsion in Palestine must go its own way. Also in that neighborhood, convulsions do happen. Within this century, Armenians have been massacred, and the Greeks have been driven from Asia Minor, which was their homeland for nigh three thousand years.

Most British statesmen are keenly aware that they are primarily a coordinating agency, exercising police control, and seeking political structures with intrinsic survival power. Some English statesmen of vigorous decisiveness forget this role; they try to decide and impose. They are the failures in modern English history, much beloved by vivid intellectuals. Cromwell in Ireland is an outstanding example in the past, and Carlyle was an admiring intellectual.

The second element in political success is "compromise." The essence of freedom requires political compromise. A clash of interests arises when the social system concerned involves a divergence of aim; compromise means an endeavor to adjust these differences so that the social life shall offer the largest spread of satisfactions. Political solutions devoid of compromise are failures from the ideal of statesmanship.

The tradition of Jewish life does not include any large experience in the political management of the societies throughout which it is spread. Jewish thought naturally concentrates on specific ideals, conceived in the abstract, devoid of compromise and of the requisites for survival.

This characteristic, combined with the ability of the race, is the reason for the incalculable services of the Jews to civilization. They supplied ideals beyond conventional habits. At the same time it explains the failure of the race throughout its long history to maintain stable political structures. Jewish history, beyond all histories, is composed of tragedies.

Christianity was founded in Jerusalem, proclaiming ideals beyond the customary habits of the world. The Christian Church, which gave Europe its modern civilization, was seated in Rome, where the long habit of imperial rule adjusted ideals to immediate necessities. Christianity gained its genius from Judaea, and its survival power from the Roman Empire. In the result, Christianity was a Jewish creation interfused with Roman stability.

To-day another tragedy is crucifying the Jewish race. The work of rescue is again vivified by a prophetic hope—the ideal of a Jewish National Home in the central region of its history.

There is always a condition attached to the success of any ideal seeking embodiment in historic reality. The condition in this case is the cooperation of the Mahometan world. There is good reason to anticipate success; Jewish cooperation was a factor in the great period of Mahometan brilliance. In the present remodeling of the Mahometan world, Jewish skills give the exact assistance that the populations require: 'Jewish learning can mould Mahometan learning to assimilate modern knowledge; Palestine is placed exactly at the sensitive point where the Western world touches Mahometan life.

The University of Jerusalem, technological schools, modes of agriculture and of manufacture, should extend their influence throughout the Near East. Also care should be taken to avoid the indiscriminate extension of European legal ideas into a social life to which they are alien. Crude notions of personal ownership, or of state dominance, fail to apply to the subtleties of tribal life. A sensitive response to the real facts of the life around is required. The simplicities of abstract thought must be shunned.

These warnings are commonplace. Unfortunately they are required.

In the adjustment of Jews and Arabs, one-sided bargains are to be dreaded. They spell disaster in the future. The hope of statesmen should be to elicit notions of mutual service and of the interweaving of habits so that the diversity of populations should issue in the fulfillment of the varied subconscious claims on life.

There is a new world waiting to be born, stretched along the eastern shores of the Mediterranean and the western shores of the Indian Ocean. The condition for its life is the fusion of Mahometan and Jewish populations, each with their own skills and their own memories, and their own ideals.

War can protect; it cannot create. Indeed, war adds to the brutality that frustrates creation. The protection of war should be the last resort in the slow progress of mankind towards its far-off ideals.

VI

The Importance of Friendly Relations
Between England and the United States

WHEN the President of the University Association of American Women did me the honour to ask me to speak today upon the importance of friendly relations between England and the United States, she chose one of the most biased persons whom she could possibly have hit upon. I am an Englishman, passionately loving my own country; and I am living here in Cambridge, among American friends who daily by their charm and kindness evoke every warm feeling of attachment. How can I help believing that the two countries should cherish the closest relations of friendship?

But I will try to express the general importance of friendship between England and the United States in a way which is independent of my own feelings, though it explains them.

By friendship I do not mean that on either side there should be imitation, or in any respect a blurring of those special traditions which go to form that unique claim to affection which a great country makes upon its citizens. We shall best understand each other when it is clearly understood that Englishmen intend to remain English, and that Americans intend to remain American.

It is true that in its origin this nation was founded by men of English blood, with English habits of thought, who carried with them across the ocean English institutions, English laws, and English literature. But even in your origin, you started as a protest against the tendencies which were then dominant in England. Also amid novel circumstances and in the course of three hundred years, you have modified those traditions and those institutions in a way which is peculiarly your own. America, as was originally the case in England, has grown by the addition of immigrants from nearly all the great European nations. Accordingly, your racial inheritance, taken as a whole, though very analogous to that of Great Britain, having regard to the mixture of races there, yet is not the same.

But, when all these qualifications have been made, the overwhelming fact remains that the United States of today, and the England of today, are parallel, though diverse, developments of one great tradition of civilised life. You have only got to live most of your life in one country, and then go and live in the other, and you will find that, amid all the obvious differences, there is a fundamental likeness which springs from a common deep-down basis of assumption governing conduct in both countries. Americans in London feel very much at home; and nobody in England thinks it other than natural that they should so feel. I am not speaking of the chances of a casual visit of a few days, but of those who stay long enough to know us. Also I can testify from my own experience how much of a home America can be to an Englishman. It is not merely the common language. The sort of things you think, the sort of things you enjoy, and the sort of things you do, are all things that one can easily in imagination put across as coming from one's friends at home. Amid all the difference, one soon finds that in spirit one has not travelled very far.

It is impossible in a few sentences to express what is meant by a kinship of spirit. For that fullness of understanding I can only refer you to individual experiences, and to the naturalness which on either side of the ocean we find in our common literature. English and American literatures have their distinctions; but, like the nations themselves, they are parallel developments from the same root.

There are, however, a few outstanding ideals held in common by both peoples, which I do wish to mention. These ideals are of the utmost importance for the world in general; and the possibility of their effectiveness throughout the world depends on the friendly rivalry between the United States and Great Britain in their exhibition.

Fundamentally, this ideal is the belief in the plain good sense of well-meaning people, freely organising themselves, under the protection of equal laws, for the various purposes of life. We do not want to be drilled into obedience. We want to go about our own affairs, and our own enjoyments, in free, peaceful association with our fellows. It is the ideal natural to an energetic and adventurous community. We are not herds to be driven, and used for the schemes of supermen. We believe in the importance of shaping our ends in life under the guidance of a strong moral purpose. In the region of national policy, we believe that the best action for the nation's welfare will be controlled by our sense of what is right and fair as between man and man. We hold that such a policy is not only right in itself; but is also in the long run, the best and subtlest policy for our nation's good. America and

England stand for the ideal that nations, though they cannot wholly disregard the occasional necessity for force, must ordinarily depend upon the persuasions of reason, and upon the credit that comes from fair dealing and reliability. They believe in the moral governance of the world, by which it has been decreed that in the end, force and brutality revenge themselves upon those nations which depend upon such violence. In their internal policy, these countries have invented the only two methods of free democratic government which are adapted to the modern world.

In their external policy, they are the two great nations who most consistently have been ready to submit great issues to peaceful arbitration, and who have most consistently aimed at limiting their armed forces. For example, at the present moment the embodied English army is 215,000 men. Of this army, there are about 30,000 men in India, which is practically a continent in itself, inhabited by a population numbering 350,000,000 people. Our great fortresses which are dispersed along our oceanic trade routes require some thousands for their garrisons. You must remember that the food supply in England is never more than that sufficient for a few weeks' consumption. In an absolutely literal sense, our daily bread depends upon enabling the navy to keep open these oceanic trade routes. Again, the total number in the army includes the half-trained recruits. Finally, some thousands are in Egypt, in the neighborhood of the Suez Canal which is the highway of our communication with Australia and the East. I think that you will agree that we have cut the numbers very fine.

The peculiar non-military temper of the two peoples is due to the good fortune of their circumstances. So far as their communications with other nations are concerned, they are both of them predominantly oceanic peoples. They have no experience of the horrors of foreign invasion.

This question of the sea-borne lines of communication brings me to another point. England is the president of a commonwealth of kindred nations, which have been founded by the adventures of its over-dense population. It is a commonwealth of democratic nations, each with its own marked and increasing national peculiarities. Each of these nations is also oceanic for the greater part of its foreign communications. Each of them is marked non-military, and is anxious to follow the lines of peaceful development.

The common interest of all these nations is a peaceful world, open for the mutual benefit of enterprise, in material goods, in art, and in thought. The general interests of the British Commonwealth, and the general interests of the United States, are identical. In particular matters there may be clashes of policy, to be adjusted by reasonable discussion and accommodation. But in general aims there should be complete community of purpose, and courtesy of interchange.

On this point, England and English statesmen are unanimous. The general aims of the two nations, and their general social development are so exactly on parallel lines, that no responsible Englishman has any other thought than to adjust the lines of policy of the two powers, so as to work in common for an orderly world of the open door and with equal opportunity.

In thinking of England, you cannot exaggerate in your estimate of how greatly the thoughts of English statesmen are controlled by the consideration of the relation of England to the great Dominions which form the component parts of the Commonwealth. It is the vital obsession which is the key to the whole foreign policy of the country. In the middle of the nineteenth century, these Dominions were colonies and were in the background of English thought. Today, they are in the foreground. The colonial period has passed: and the Dominions have taken their places as nations, growing into a greatness whose limits in the future have not yet been defined. The efforts of statesmen are now directed to discover that elastic bond which shall preserve the advantages of intimate friendly cooperation, without curbing the growth of national individuality.

I have mentioned some general thoughts which rise to our minds when we think of friendship between England and the United States. Now I want to speak more directly to the American Youth who form the chief part of this audience. In the next sixty years, you are going to live through a wonderful period of your country's history. Nothing can prevent the United States from being the greatest nation in the World, both in wealth and in military power. You are secure from attack; you have endless resources; you are self-contained; you have a brave and intelligent population. All the elements of power are yours. It could only be matched by a united and a militarised Western Europe; or, in some remote time, by a renovated China, or Russia. But for your life-time, certainly the power is yours.

How is that power going to be used?

You, the young Americans to-day, will be the men responsible for the way in which the World emerges at the end of this century. You cannot shirk your responsibilities. Fate has put them upon you. If you let the wrong influences form your popular judgments, and control either your government, or your big corporations, or your art, or your literature, or your science, it is you who are to blame. You should have had the force and the energy yourselves to take the lead. Your generation will stand conspicuous at the bar of History; and History has no mercy upon those who, having the opportunity, allow themselves to be thrust aside. Above all things, a democratic State depends upon its citizens facing up to their duties. With the fate of the World depending on your actions, you cannot, you must not, fail your country.

Keep this thought in your minds: What will be said of America when this century closes?

You have a chance straight in front of you such as no nation has had before. Without deviating from what, in the long run, is your legitimate self-interest, you can lead the World into paths of sanity, and of mutual comprehension. You can be the greatest patrons of living art that the World has seen; you can keep the peace; you can introduce habits of fair international dealings, and of the deference of power to the claims of justice; you can foster international friendship by the intercourse of games, of sport, and of other occasions of mutual interest.

Every nation has its varying moods, upwards and downwards. In my own life-time, I have seen England commit errors—indeed crimes—for which there is no defence; and I have seen it rise to standards of conduct whose glory, as I believe, will stand for ever. A great people, acting on a great stage, has to make decisions amid novel circumstances. It is criminal not to know in time when some old maxim of prudent statecraft does not apply to the case immediately before you.

Nations make their great mistakes when their citizens fail in sympathy with other peoples. Every nation makes its own contribution to the life of the world. We cannot do without each other. Try and understand how the people of other nations are living; see what their difficulties are; understand what they really achieve in the way of fine conduct. Do not look upon a foreign nation as one big rival bogie. It is composed of men and women, boys and girls, just like yourselves.

Above all things I ask you to remember this—and now I am speaking as a European, just as much as an Englishman— In estimating what other peoples have done for the world, try and understand the difficulties under which they acted. I mean the limitations of power, the limitations of knowledge, the limitations of experience, the limitations of security. Also remember that often statesmen, and nations, and individuals, were warding off evils which, because they did not develop, we have now forgotten. Think of what they accomplished in the way of establishing great standards of life, and great ideals of thought. You now have your opportunity, because you inherit from Europe arts, and laws, and political philosophy, and science. You brought them with you, and they are yours by right. But when you build, as you should build, even finer ideals and better ways of life, remember that you are profiting by the labours of others, and that it is for you to see that mankind shall profit from the civilization which you create.

VII

The Education of an Englishman

WE think in generalities, but we live in detail. To make the past live, we must perceive it in detail in addition to thinking of it in generalities. In this paper I am jotting down recollections of details and generalities of boyhood in an English school, fifty years ago.

Tolstoy has written, as the first sentence of his *Anna Karenina:* "Happy families are all alike; every unhappy family is unhappy in its own way." Thus what is best in English boyhood of the period is identical with what is best in New England experience, of today or of that period. But every nation is bad in its own way. We cannot be social reformers all the time. In our off moments we view our peculiar domestic mixture of goods and evils with an affectionate tolerance of their incongruities, which we call "humour." So please remember in reading English literature that the humourous aspects of English life are in general minor symptoms of social defects.

Any account of a phase of national life must throw light on two things: (a) why the nation is as good as it is, and (b) why the nation is as bad as it is. If it be our own country which is in question, the combined complex fact is the country which we love, with its virtues and its defects.

Personal recollections are limited by personal experience. So these pages are not recollections of English education *passim;* but they are typical of one important phase, and apart from knowledge of this phase you cannot understand how England functioned during the latter sixty years of the nineteenth century. The limitations of these recollections can be defined by a reference to Anthony Trollope. His novels refer to the grown-up members of the same society. My recollections refer to the children of the families which he writes about. The fathers of the boys were archdeacons, canons, rectors in the Established Church, or officers in the Army, or small squires in the Southwest of England, or lawyers, or doctors. There was a sprinkling of boys from large commercial families.

Most of the moderate capital behind the professional families had come from commerce at no distant date. For us commerce meant trade, banking, ship-owning. Manufactures belonged to the North of England, of which our knowledge was about as vague as it was of the United States. Of course we knew about it, and it was a subject for pride as a national asset, but we did not grasp what it really meant. Anyone who comes from the North of England can reciprocate this indifference of boyhood, from the opposite end.

The school was in Dorsetshire, at Sherborne, a small town of six thousand inhabitants. At that time there were three hundred boys. We were locally termed "The King's Scholars," in allusion to the remodeling of the school in the sixteenth century by King Edward the Sixth. As time was reckoned in that district, this event was still a recent innovation. It was a blot on the scutcheon, introducing a modern vulgarity into what would otherwise have been an unbroken continuity of a thousand years.

Geography is half of character. The soil there is rich, loamy, and gravelly. The climate is formed by warm currents and warm moist winds from the South Atlantic. My own home was in the Southeast of England, where we are formed by the polar currents and Siberian winds which come down the North Sea, with interludes of South Atlantic weather from the English Channel. But the interludes in the East were the habitual climate in the West. England is the battleground for these opposed currents, polar on the eastern side, subtropical on the southwestern side. Dorsetshire was a rich agricultural district, with apple orchards, and woodlands, and ferns, and rolling grass downs. It did not matter which end of a shrub you put into the ground when planting it; the shrub was bound to grow six feet in the next year. The peasantry had an English dialect of their own, which an Easterner could hardly understand. They were a kindly folk; if a schoolboy on a country walk asked for water, he was given cider and no payment taken.

The town and school had all been founded together by Saint Aldhelm, who died in the year 709, after planting a monastery in that spot. Their importance in the scheme of things has been singularly level from that time on. Perhaps the chief importance came in the eleventh and twelfth centuries, but minor ups and downs hardly count. The most distinguished of the scholars was King Alfred. His connection with the school was mythical, but undoubted. Indeed, vague traditions of the place went back beyond Alfred and beyond Aldhelm to King Arthur, who was said to have held his court on the site of the old British earthworks, amid the neighboring downs. (Every respectable district in the West of England claims King Arthur.) Certainly when you sat there, on Cadbury Castle, on a warm summer afternoon in the quiet of the dreaming landscape, it seemed eminently probable;

and the school song accepted the tradition without question.

So far as sound was concerned, the chief elements were the school bell—a wretched tinkle by which our lives were regulated—and the magnificent bells of the big Abbey Church, which were brought from Tournai by Henry VIII when he returned from the Field of the Cloth of Gold, and given by him to the Abbey. These bells were a great factor in the moulding of the school character, the living voices of past centuries.

This aesthetic background was an essential element in the education, explanatory alike of inertia and of latent idealism. The education cannot be understood unless it is realized that it elucidated an ever-present dream world in our subconscious life.

Some of our classrooms were parts of the old monastery buildings. My own private study in the last two years at school was said to have been the Abbot's cell. The evidence was vague and devoid of documents, but while you lived there it was indubitable. The new school buildings were in the old style, and built of material from the same quarry as that which, centuries earlier, had furnished the stone for the Abbey and the Monastery. This was the Ham Hill quarry. Old Mother Shipton, a prophetess of the early nineteenth century, prophesied that the end of the world would start from Ham Hill. I disbelieve her, because sheer inertia would keep Ham Hill going long after the rest of things had disappeared. To start anything at Ham Hill would constitute a miracle overtaxing credulity.

We had plenty of evidence that things had been going on for a long time. It never entered into anybody's mind to regard six thousand years seriously as the age of mankind—not because we took up with revolutionary ideas, but because our continuity with nature was a patent, visible fact, and had been so since the days of Saint Aldhelm. There were incredible quantities of fossils about; more fossils than stones—or rather, the stones were built out of fossils, welded together.

The boys had thorough country tastes, and knew about the birds, and the ferns, and the foxes, and the gardens. Their fathers rode with the foxhounds, and so did their mothers and sisters. Those who did not hunt planted flowers in their gardens, knew all about the archaeology of the neighborhood, and read Tennyson. Browning would have bothered them. Between whiles, they achieved a good deal of patronage of their social inferiors, with more or less brutality or kindliness, according to breeding and character.

The squire of the district was a very big man, owned half the county, and daily drove his own carriage with four horses—a four-in-hand, as we call it. He was an oldish man then, but he did everything in the grand manner. He and his wife were strict evangelical church people. They must have come under the influence of their neighbor, Lord Shaftesbury, the social reformer. His estates were well managed, with great liberality. This demoralized the neighborhood, because the "Old Squire" was expected to pay for everything, and did so. He was the chairman of the Board of Governors of the school, and when he died he was succeeded by the Bishop of Salisbury. That sort of alternation had been going on from time immemorial. Nobody thought of it as old habit, or particularly cherished it for that reason; it was just the nature of things—either a Digby or the Bishop; there was no alternative. Nobody in Sherborne ever did anything explicitly because it was traditional. That is a characteristic of modern progressive societies.

The squire lived in the new castle, a Tudor building of the age of Elizabeth. The old castle was on the other side of the lake in the park. Its Norman keep was blown to pieces by Cromwell's soldiers, after it had been defended against the Parliament by the Countess Digby of that epoch. I do not know why the new castle got itself built half a century before the old castle was knocked down. But after all, the Digbys survived the Puritan soldiers, and so have their political principles of West Country Toryism. To-day the government of England is in the hands of West Country men with an industrial experience—Baldwin and Austen Chamberlain—who are endeavoring to adapt the Digby traditions to modern times. Chamberlain is Birmingham and Worcestershire, and Baldwin is a Shropshire man who has been a large ironmaster. When he was first Prime Minister, some of his workmen made a pilgrimage to Downing Street and held a bean-feast there.

In the old-world woodlands and orchards of the West Country, with its reminiscent landscape, a secret has been whispered down the generations: the secret of governing England in days when kindly sense and tolerance are required to heal its wounds.

The staff of the school, the headmaster and his colleagues, were all strong Liberals, classical scholars, and modernist churchmen. This was in strict accordance with the Rugby tradition, which had been established by Thomas Arnold, a full generation earlier. The Tory squires of the neighborhood, who governed the school, were conscientious men, and knew how a gentleman should be educated. According to the tradition, which stretched really beyond Arnold, this could only be done efficiently by gentlemen who had read the classics with sufficient zeal to convert them to the principles of Athenian democracy and Roman tyrannicide.

We were taught a good deal of history, very thoroughly so far as it went. But it was characteristically limited according to the prejudices shared equally by the Liberal schoolmasters, the Tory parents, and their children who were the scholars. Our reading was closely limited to those periods of history which, if we might trust out national pride, were closely analogous to our own. We did not want to explain the origin of anything. We wanted to read about people like ourselves, and to imbibe their ideals. When the Bible said, "All these things happened unto them for ensamples," we did not need a higher critic to tell us what was meant or how it came to be written. It was just how we felt.

For example, in Roman history we stopped short at the death of Julius Caesar. Freedom was over then. A gentleman could no longer say what he liked in the House of Lords or in the House of Commons—that is to say, in the Roman Senate or to the citizens in the Forum. Strictly speaking, we ought to have stopped when Caesar crossed the Rubicon; but human nature is always illogical, and we—that is to say, masters and scholars—were urged on by curiosity to see how it ended, and also by secret sympathy with Caesar, who was very like a great English landed magnate of cultivated mind and of sporting tastes, contesting his county parliamentary constituency, with a good chance of being unseated for bribery and corruption. Pompey was unpopular; he lacked the West Country touch. Cicero needed no explanation—he was the Roman substitute for a Lord Chancellor.

These things were not explained to us: the facts spoke for themselves. We read Tacitus and enjoyed his epigrams, though they were hard to translate into English terse enough to satisfy our masters, and we were not allowed to use English versions. Tacitus carried our sympathies along with him in his denunciation of a state of society which had lost all close analogy to the British Constitution. So we made no study of Imperial Rome; it lacked political interest.

I am not wandering from my subject. I am endeavoring to

explain the direct relevance of a classical education half a century ago to the state of mind of an English schoolboy. The prayer which one of us in turn had to read daily in the school chapel told us that we were being trained "to serve God in Church and State," and we never conceived life in any other terms. The competitive conception of modern industry was entirely absent from our minds; also we were ignorant—comparatively ignorant—of the peculiar problems incident in such a society. The terms in which the Greeks and the Romans thought were good enough for us. What had not been said in Greek on political philosophy had not been said at all.

The Greeks reigned supreme in our minds. Roman gladiators, Roman debauchery, Roman grandiosity, the difficulties of writing Latin prose in the style of Cicero, the absence of a definite article in the Latin language, the Roman Emperors, and the Popes of Rome, all contributed to a feeling that Rome lacked any true intimate affinity with us. Looking backward, I think that our instincts were right. The social tone of Dorsetshire in the eighteen-seventies was really very different from that of Rome at any time of its history, despite the analogies which caught our interest.

But Athens was the ideal city, which for two centuries had shown the world what life could be. I do not affirm that our image of Athens was true to the facts. It was something much better; it was alive. The Athenian navy and the British navy together ruled the seas of our imaginations. It was not oceans that we thought of, but narrow seas. Oceans are the discovery of the last half-century, so far as English schoolboys are concerned, and putting Robinson Crusoe aside as the exception to prove the rule. Our navy has never ruled the oceans. It ruled the seas. It caught its enemies rounding capes, or moored in bays, just as the

Greeks did. Cape Trafalgar, Cape St. Vincent, and Aboukir Bay were read into Greek history. In those days, half a century ago, our main fleet was in the Mediterranean just where the Greek fleets sailed; and Russia was to us what Persia was to the Greeks. Scholars may demur to this analogy; but I am talking of school-boys fifty years ago.

Herodotus and Thucydides, with Xenophon on the Ten Thousand, were the successful authors. We all of us cherished a secret hope of traveling in the East. The East then meant the eastern Mediterranean, including Syria and Egypt. Years ago, two twin brothers—my uncles, as it happens—met by accident in a back street of Damascus, neither knowing that the other was out of England. Happy men! They were traveling in the East.

Archaeology and learning were secondary matters then, and, as I strongly suspect, are so now to many English archaeologists. It was the flavor of the East that we hungered after, the product of our classical education. To understand what I mean, read Kinglake's *Eothen;* it is short and very amusing. It is redolent of English mentality during the mid-nineteenth century.

The Greek insistence on the golden mean and on the virtue of moderation entered into our philosophy of statesmanship, sometimes reenforcing our natural stupidity, sometimes moderating our national arrogance. We conceived India through our knowledge of the East derived from the Greeks. Thus we took an immense interest in Alexander the Great. We forgot the loss of Greek liberty in the thrilling spectacle of a small European army making its way through a vast Eastern Empire. In Alexander at Issus we saw Clive at Plassey.

Decidedly, half a century ago a classical education had a very real relevance to the future lives of these English boys. Among the boys at that small school from 1870 to 1880 were a future commander-in-chief in India, a future general commanding in the Madras Presidency, a future bishop of all southern India. "To serve God in Church and State" was no idle form of words to set before them.

Our school course was a curious mixture of imaginative appeal and precise, detailed knowledge. We had no interest in foreign languages. It was Latin and Greek that we had to know. They were not foreign languages; they were just Latin and Greek; nothing of importance in the way of ideas could be presented in any other way. Thus we read the New Testament in Greek. At school—except in chapel, which did not count—I never heard of anyone reading it in English. It would suggest an uncultivated religious state of mind. We were very religious, but with that moderation natural to people who take their religion in Greek.

The difficulty as to the Old Testament was surmounted by reading the Septuagint in class on Sunday afternoons, though the lower forms had to descend to the vulgarity of the King James Bible. In this Greek presentation of religion the passion for accurate philology sometimes overcame the religious interest. I remember the headmaster stopping a boy who, when translating into English before the assembled class, reeled off the familiar phrase, "Alas, alas, the glory of Israel hath departed," with "No, no, laddie: The glory of Israel has gone away as a colonist."

A few days ago the head of a Canadian university called on me. He turned out to be from the same school; he went there the term after I left. We called to mind these Septuagint lessons, and agreed that in some way they were among the valuable elements of our school training. The Platonizing Jews of Alexandria are mixed in my mind with monastery buildings in Dorsetshire on warm Sunday afternoons in May. When I try to recall how we thought of the Jews, I think that it is accurately summed up in the statement that we believed them to be inspired, but otherwise unimportant.

We studied some mathematics, very well taught; some science and some French, both very badly taught; also some plays of Shakespeare, which were the worst feature of all. To this day I cannot read *King Lear,* having had the advantage of studying it accurately at school. The failure of the science and of the French was not the fault of the masters. An angel from Heaven could not have persuaded us to take them seriously. Again I am not defending us, but am recording facts.

There was a strict monitorial system. In fact, the discipline out of the classroom depended entirely on the head boys in each house. These boys were chosen merely according to their standing in the intellectual life of the school. If the prefects were also athletic and of high character, the system worked very well; otherwise it worked very badly. In my own schooldays, for about half the time it worked badly and for the other half extremely well. There was some teasing, but no gross bullying. When I was "head of the school," I remember caning a boy before the whole school for stealing. Again I am recording, and not defending. I consulted the headmaster privately, and he told me that the alternative was expulsion.

In respect to games we were much more independent than modern English schoolboys or undergraduates at any American university. We had lovely playing fields surrounded by intimate scenery such as, in all the world, only the West of England can provide. We managed the games ourselves, and trained ourselves. We played cricket, and football, and fives, because we enjoyed those games and for no other reason. Efficiency, what crimes are committed in thy name! To-day, throughout English schools, the games are supervised by the younger masters. Fifty years ago at Sherborne no master either played a game or interfered with advice, except by the express invitation of the boy who was captain of the games. We were not efficient; we enjoyed ourselves. Also, perhaps in consequence of that freedom from supervision, we were on the best of terms with the masters, and were always pleased when any of the younger members of the staff accepted our invitation to play, an invitation which was regularly forthcoming on every occasion.

In the particular "house"—that is to say, set of dormitories— where I lived, there were ninety boys and four baths. Again I am recording and not defending. Of course there were washbasins in our bedrooms, the water being put there in jugs. Labor was cheap in those days, and plumbing was barely in its infancy. Fifty years before that time the boys washed under a pump in the school yard. They also managed to serve God in Church and State, so little are some things affected by modern conveniences.

We rose—nominally—at 6:30 A.M. and were in chapel at 7 A.M., if our state of dress, or undress, enabled us to pass the prefect at the chapel door. If not, we had to write out some lines in Greek. I remember cuffing a big boy over the head because I found him twisting the arm of a small boy; but I apologized afterward, because I found that the small boy had called his elder "a captain of Barbary apes"; this was unpermissible insolence in the school world.

Altogether we were a happy set of boys, receiving a deplorably narrow education to fit us for the modern world. But I will disclose one private conviction, based upon no confusing research, that, as a training in political imagination, the Harvard School of Politics and of Government cannot hold a candle to the old-fashioned English classical education of half a century ago.

VIII

Harvard: The Future

I

In the tercentenary celebrations of this summer, Harvard marks the accomplishment of its process of growth. About twenty-five years for a man and about three hundred years for a university are the periods required for the attainment of mature stature. The history of Harvard is no longer to be construed primarily in terms of growth, but in terms of effectiveness.

I am talking of effectiveness in the wide world, of impress on the course of events, without which civilized humanity would not be as in fact it is. In the Cambridge of England, the first college was founded in the year 1284, and Emmanuel College in the year 1584. The English university was then grown up. Within the next one hundred and fifty years there occurred a brilliant period—*the* brilliant period—of European civilization. It staged a decisive episode in the drama of human life. In this episode the English university played no mean part, from Edmund Spenser and Francis Bacon at the outset to Newton and Dryden at the close. Among other things, Cambridge helped to contribute Milton, Cromwell, and Harvard University.

The term "European civilization" is now a misnomer, for the

centre of gravity has shifted. Civilization haunts the borders of waterways. The shores of the Mediterranean and the western coasts of Europe are cases in point. But nowadays, relatively to our capacities, the dimensions of the world have shrunk, and the Atlantic Ocean plays the same role as the European seas in the former centuries. The total result is that the North American shores of the Atlantic are in the central position to influence the adventures of mankind, from East to West and from North to South. The static aspects of things are measured from the meridian of Greenwich; but the world will rotate around the long line of American shores.

What is the influence of Harvard to mean in the immediate future, originating thought and feeling during the next fifty years, or during the next one hundred and fifty years? Harvard is one of the outstanding universities in the very centre of human activity. At the present moment it is magnificently equipped. It has enjoyed nigh seventy years of splendid management. A new epoch is opening in the world. There are new potentialities, new hopes, new fears. The old scales of relative quantitative importance have been inverted. New qualitative experiences are developing. And yet, beneath all the excitement of novelty, with its discard and rejection, the basic motives for human action remain, the old facts of human nature clothed in a novelty of detail. What is the task before Harvard?

It will be evident that in this summary presentation of the cultural problem the word "Harvard" is to be taken partly in its precise designation of a particular institution and partly as a symbolic reference to the university system throughout the Eastern states of this country. A closely intertwined group of institutions, the outcome of analogous impulses, has in the last three hundred years gradually developed, from Charlottesville to Baltimore, from Baltimore to Boston, and from Boston to Chicago. Of these institutions some are larger and some are smaller, some are in cities and some are in country places, some are older and some are younger. But each of them has the age of the group, as moulded by this cultural impulse. The fate of the intellectual civilization of the world is to-day in the hands of this group— for such time as it can effectively retain the sceptre. And to-day there is no rival. The Aegean coast line had its chance and made use of it; Italy had its chance and made use of it; France, England, Germany, had their chance and made use of it. Today the Eastern American states have their chance. What use will they make of it? The question has two answers. Once Babylon had its chance and produced the Tower of Babel. The University of Paris fashioned the intellect of the Middle Ages. Will Harvard fashion the intellect of the twentieth century?

II

We cannot usefully discuss the organization of universities, considered as educational institutions, apart from a preliminary survey of the general character of human knowledge, and of some special features of modern life. Such a survey elicits perplexities which have troubled learning from the earliest days of the Greeks to the present moment. By introducing implicit assumptions in respect to these problems, it is possible to arrive at almost any doctrine respecting university organization.

In the first place, there is the division into certainty and probability. Some items we are certain about, others are matters of opinion. There is an obvious common sense about this doctrine, and its enunciation goes back to Plato. The class of certainties falls into two subdivisions. In one subdivision are certain large general truths—for example, the multiplication table, axioms as to quantitative "more or less"—and certain aesthetic and moral presuppositions. In the other subdivision are momentary discriminations of one's own state of mind: for example, a state of feeling—happiness at this moment; and for another example, an item of sense perception—that colored shape experienced at this moment. But recollection and interpretation are both deceitful. Thus this latter subdivision just touches certainty and then loses it. There is mere imitation of certainty.

In the class of probabilities, there are to be found all our judgments as to the goings on of this world of temporal succession, except so far as these happenings are qualified by the certainties whenever they are relevant.

I repeat my affirmation that, in some sense or other, this characterization of human knowledge is indubitable. No one doubts the multiplication table; also everyone admits that a witness on the witness stand can only produce fallible evidence, which the judicial authorities endeavor to assess, again only fallibly.

The bearing of these doctrines on the procedures of education cannot be missed. In the first place: Develop intellectual activities by a knowledge of the certain truths, so far as they are largely applicable to human life. In the second place: Train the understanding of each student to assess probable knowledge in respect to those types of occurrences which for any reason will be of major importance in the exercise of his activities. In the third place: Give him adequate knowledge of the possibilities of aesthetic and moral satisfaction which are open to a human being, under conditions relevant to his future life.

So far there is no disagreement. Unfortunately, exactly at this point our difficulties commence. This is the reason why the prefatory analysis was necessary. These difficulties are best explained by a slight reference to the history of thought, stretching from Greece to William James.

Plato was a voluminous writer, and apparently all his works have come down to us. They constitute a discussion of the various types of certain knowledge, of probable knowledge, and of aesthetic and moral ideas. This discussion, viewed as elucidating the above-mentioned classification of knowledge which is to be the basis of education, was a complete failure. He failed to make clear what was certain; and where he was certain, we disagree with him. He failed to make clear the relationship of things certain to things probable; and where he thought he was clear, we disagree with him. He failed to make clear the moral and aesthetic ends of life; and where he thought he was clear, we disagree with him. No two of his dialogues are completely consistent with each other. No two modern scholars agree as to what any one dialogue exactly means. This failure of Plato is the great fact dominating the history of European thought.

Also this failure was typical. It stretches through every topic of human interest. Every single generalization respecting mathematical physics, which I was taught at the University of Cambridge during my student period from the years 1880 to 1885, has now been abandoned in the sense in which it was then held. The words are retained, but with different meanings.

The truth is that this beautiful subdivision of human knowledge, whether you make it twofold or threefold, goes up in smoke as soon as you try to fasten upon it any exact meaning. As a vague preliminary guide, it is useful. But when you trust it without reserve, it violates the conditions of human experience. This history of thought is largely concerned with the records of clear-headed men insisting that they at last have discovered some clear, adequately expressed, indubitable truths. If clear-headed men throughout the ages would only agree with each other, we might cease to be puzzled. Alas, that is a comfort denied to us.

III

The outcome of this brief survey is so fundamental in its relevance to education that it must be elucidated further by considering it in reference to two topics—Mathematics, and the Abiding Importance of Plato.

The science of Mathematics is the very citadel of the doctrine of certainty. It is unnecessary to bring the large developments of the subject into this discussion. Let us consider the multiplication table. This table is concerned with simple interrelations of cardinal numbers, as for example, "Twice three" is "six." Nothing can be more certain. But a little question arises: What are cardinal numbers? There is no universally accepted answer to this question. In fact, it is the battle ground of a controversy. The innocent suggestions which occur to us are traps which lead us into self-contradictions or into other puzzles. The notion of number is obviously concerned with the concept of a class, or a group, of many things. It expresses the special sort of many-ness in question. Unfortunately the notion of a class is beset with ambiguities leading to logical traps. We then have recourse to the fundamental notions of logic, and again encounter a contest of dissentient opinions. Logic is the chosen resort of clear-headed people, severally convinced of the complete adequacy of their doctrines. It is such a pity that they cannot agree with each other.

Analogous perplexities arise in respect to the fundamental notions of other mathematical topics: for example, the meaning of the notions of a point, of a line, and of a straight line. There is great confidence and no agreement.

Thus the palmary instances of human certainty, Logic and Mathematics, have given way under the scrutiny of two thousand years. To-day we have less apparent ground for certainty than had Plato and Aristotle. The natural rebound from this conclusion is skepticism. Trust your reflexes, says the skeptic, and do not seek to understand. Your reflexes are the outcome of routine. Your emotions are modes of reception of the process. There is no understanding, because there is nothing to understand.

Complete skepticism involves an aroma of self-destruction. It seems as the negation of experience. It craves for an elegy on the passing of rational knowledge—the beautiful youth drowned in the Sea of Vacuity.

The large practical effect of skepticism is gross acquiescence in what is immediate and obvious. Postponement, subtle interweaving, delicacies of adjustment, wide coordination, moral restraint, the whole artistry of civilization, all presuppose understanding. And without understanding they are meaningless.

Thus, in practice, skepticism always means some knowledge, but not too much. It is indeed evident that our knowledge is limited. But the traditional skepticism is a reaction against an imperfect view of human knowledge.

It is in respect to this limitation of knowledge that the ancient division into certainties and probabilities is so misleading. It suggests that we have a perfectly clear indication of the items in question, and are either certain or uncertain as to the existence of some definite connection between them. For example, it presupposes that we have a perfectly clear indication of the numbers 2 and 3 and 6, and are either certain or uncertain as to whether twice three is six.

The fact is the other way round. We are very vague as to the meanings of 1, and 2, and 3, and 5, and 6. But we want to determine these meanings so as to preserve the relations, "six is one more than five" and "twice three is six." In other words, we are more clear as to the interrelations of the numbers than as to their separate individual characters. We use the interrelations as a step toward the determinations of the things related.

This is an instance of the general truth, that our progress in clarity of knowledge is primarily from the composition to its ingredients. The very meaning of the notion of definition is the use of composition for the purpose of indication.

The important characterization of knowledge is in respect to clarity and vagueness.

The reason for this dominance of vagueness and clarity in respect to the problem of knowledge is that the world is not made up of independent things, each completely determinate in abstraction from all the rest. Contrast is of the essence of character. In its happy instances contrast is harmony; in its unhappy instances contrast is confusion. Our experience is dominated by composite wholes, more or less clear in the focus, and more or less vague in the penumbra, and with the whole shading off into umbral darkness which is ignorance. But throughout the whole, alike in the focal regions, the penumbral regions, and the umbral regions, there is baffling mixture of clarity and vagueness.

The primary weapon is analysis. And analysis is the evocation of insight by the hypothetical suggestions of thought, and the evocation of thought by the activities of direct insight. In this process the composite whole, the interrelations, and the things related, concurrently emerge into clarity.

One of the most interesting facts in the psychology of young students at the present time is the abiding interest of the platonic writings. From the point of view of displaying the sharp distinction between the certainties and the opinions involved in human knowledge, Plato failed. But he gave an unrivaled display of the human mind in action, with its ferment of vague obviousness, of hypothetical formulation, of renewed insight, of discovery of relevant detail, of partial understanding of final conclusion, with its disclosure of deeper problems as yet unsolved. There we find exposed to our view the problem of education as it should dominate a university. Knowledge is a process, adding content and control to the flux of experience. It is the function of a university to initiate its students in the exercise of this process of knowledge.

IV

The problem before Harvard is set by the termination of an epoch in European culture. For three centuries European learning has employed itself in a limited definite task. It was a necessary task and an important one. Scholars, in science and in literature, have been brilliantly successful. But they have finished that task—at least for the time, although every task is resumed after the lapse of some generations. However, for the moment, the trivialization of the traditional scholarship is the note of our civilization.

The fundamental presupposition behind learning has been that of the possession of clear ideas, as starting points for all expression and all theory. The problem has been to weave these ideas into compound structures with the attributes either of truth, or of beauty, or of moral elevation. There was presumed to be no difficulty in framing sentences in which each word and each phrase had an exact meaning. The only topics for discussion were whether the sentence when framed was true or false, beautiful or ugly, moral or shocking. European learning was founded on the dictionary; and splendid dictionaries were produced. With the culmination of the dictionaries the epoch has ended. For this reason, all the dictionaries of all the languages have failed to provide for the expression of the full human experience.

The ultimate cause for this characteristic of European learning was that from the close of the dark ages civilization had been progressing with the gradual recovery of the subtle, many-sided literature of the classical civilization. Thought then had the character of a recovery of the wide variety of meanings embedded in Greek and Hellenistic written literature. The result was that everything that a modern scholar thought could have been immediately understood by Thucydides, or Democritus, or Plato, or Aristotle, or Archimedes. Any one of these men would have understood Newton's Laws of Motion at a glance. These laws were a new structure of old ideas. Perhaps Aristotle would have shied at Newton's first law. But he would have understood it. Any one of these men would have understood the American Declaration of Independence. There is nothing in the Constitution of the United States to puzzle them. Perhaps the addition of these five sages to an august tribunal might even facilitate the elucidation of its applications.

The conception of mind and matter, of motion in space, of individual rights, of the rights of social groups—the world of tragedy, and of joy, and of heroism—was thoroughly familiar to the ancients, and its obvious interrelations were expressed in language, and discussed, and rediscussed. Throughout the last three or four centuries the notion of learning was the discussion of the ways of the world with the linguistic tools derived from the past. This procedure of learning was the basis of progress from the simplicities of the dark ages to the modern civilization.

For this reason a narrow convention as to learning, and as to the procedures of institutions connected with it, has developed. Tidiness, simplicity, clarity, exactness, are conceived as characteristics of the nature of things, as in human experience. It is presupposed that a university is engaged in imparting exact, clear knowledge. Lawyers are apt to presuppose that legal documents have an exact meaning, even with the absence of commas.

Thus, to a really learned man, matter exists in test tubes, animals in cages, art in museums, religion in churches, knowledge in libraries.

It is easy to sneer. But there is a problem here—a very difficult problem; and the success of Harvard depends upon maintaining a proper interweaving of its intricacies. The development of learning, and the success of education, require selection. The human mind can only deal with limited topics, which exclude the vague immensity of nature. Thus the tradition of learning is the solid ground upon which the university must be founded in respect to both sides of its activity—namely, the enlargement of knowledge and the training of youth.

The real problem is to adjust the activities of the learned institution so as to suffuse them with suggestiveness. Human nature loses its most precious quality when it is robbed of its sense of things beyond, unexplored and yet insistent. Mankind owes its progress beyond the iron limits of custom to the fact that, compared to the animals, men are amateurs. "You Greeks are always children" is the taunt from Learning to Suggestiveness.

Learning is sensible, straightforward, and clear, if only you keep at bay the suggestiveness of things. This clarity is delusive, and is shot through and through with controversy. The traditional attitude of scholars is to choose a side, and to keep the enemy at bay by exposing their errors. Of course, in the clash of doc-

trine we must base thoughts and actions on those modes of statement which seem to express the larger truth. But it is fatal to
dismiss antagonistic doctrines, supported by anybody of evidence,
as simply wrong. Inconsistent truths—that is, truths in the sense
of conformity to some evidence—are seed beds of suggestiveness.
The progress which they suggest lies at the very root of knowledge. It is concerned with the recasting of the fundamental notions on which the structure is built. The suggestion does not
primarily concern a new conclusion. Fundamental progress has
to do with the reinterpretation of basic ideas.

At this point, the problem has only been half stated. Experience does not occur in the clothing of verbal phrases. It involves clashes of emotion, and unspoken revelations of the
nature of things. Revelation is the primary characterization of
the process of knowing. The traditional theory of education is
to secure youth and its teachers from revelation. It is dangerous
for youth, and confusing to teachers. It upsets the accepted coordinations of doctrine.

Revelation is the enlargement of clarity. It is not a deduction,
though it may issue from a deduction. The dictionaries are very
weak upon this point.

V

Without doubt, in its preliminary stages education is concerned with the introduction of order into the mind of the young
child. Experience starts as a "blooming, buzzing confusion."
Order introduces enlargement, significance, importances, delicacies of perception. For long years, the major aspect of education is the reduction of confusion to order, and the provision of
weapons for this purpose.

And yet, even at the beginning of school life, it has been found necessary to interfuse the introduction of order with the enjoyment of enterprise. The balance is difficult to hold. But it is well known that education as mere imposed order of "things known" is a failure. The initial stages of reading, writing, and arithmetic should be suffused with revelation.

At the other end of education, during the university period, there is undoubtedly the excitement of novel knowledge—volumes of words. But an inversion has entered upon the stage. The child has to be taught the words that correspond to the things; the senior at college has lost the things that correspond to the words. His mind is occupied by literary scenery; by doctrines derived from books; by experiments of a selected character, with selected materials, and such that irrelevancies are neglected. Even his games are organized. Novel impulse is frowned upon at the bridge table, on the football field, and on the river. No member of a crew is praised for the rugged individuality of his rowing.

The question is how to introduce the freedom of nature into the orderliness of knowledge. The ideal of universities, with staff and students shielded from the contemplation of the sporadic life around them, will produce a Byzantine civilization, surviving for a thousand years without producing any idea fundamentally new.

There is no one recipe. It is an obvious suggestion to collect an able, vigorous faculty and give it a free hand, with every encouragement. This principle of university management has been no news at Harvard since its foundation. Also the environment of New England facilitates its practice, by producing both the men and the requisite atmosphere. It is not as simple to follow this suggestion as it looks. For half a century, on both sides of the Atlantic, I have been concerned with appointments. Nothing is more difficult than to distinguish between a loud voice and vigor, or a flow of words and originality, or mental instability and genius; or a big book and fruitful learning. Also the work requires dependable men. But if you are swayed too heavily by this admirable excellence, you will gather a faculty which can be depended upon for being commonplace.

Curiously enough, the achievements of the faculty do not depend on the exact judiciousness of each appointment. In a vigorous society, ability, in the sense of capacity for high achievement, is fairly widespread. Undoubtedly it can only be ascribed to a minority; but this minority is larger than it is conventional to estimate. The real question is to transmute the potency for achievement into the actuality of achievement. The instrument for this purpose is the stimulus of the atmosphere. In other words, we come back to suggestiveness.

Knowledge should never be familiar. It should always be contemplated either under the aspect of novel application, or under the aspect of skepticism as to the extent of its application, or under the aspect of development of its consequences, or under the aspect of eliciting the fundamental meanings which it presupposes, or under the aspect of a guide in the adventures of life, or under the aspect of the aesthetic of its interwoven relationships, or under the aspect of the miraculous history of its discovery. But no one should remain blankly content with the mere knowledge that "twice three is six"—apart from all suggestion of relevant activity.

What the faculty have to cultivate is activity in the presence of knowledge. What the students have to learn is activity in the presence of knowledge.

This discussion rejects the doctrine that students should first learn passively, and then, having learned, should apply knowledge. It is a psychological error. In the process of learning there should be present, in some sense or other, a subordinate activity of application. In fact, the applications are part of the knowledge. For the very meaning of the things known is wrapped up in their relationships beyond themselves. Thus unapplied knowledge is knowledge shorn of its meaning.

The careful shielding of a university from the activities of the world around is the best way to chill interest and to defeat progress. Celibacy does not suit a university. It must mate itself with action.

There again a problem arises. The mere scattered happenings of daily affairs are veiled from our analysis. So far as we can see, they are chance issues. The real stimulation arises from the discovery of coordinated theory illustrated in coordinated fact; and the further discovery that the fact stretches so far beyond the theory, disclosing affiliations undreamed of by learning.

VI

The picture of a university now forms itself before us. There is the central body of faculty and students, engaged in learning, elaborating, criticizing, and appreciating the varied structure of existing knowledge. This structure is supported by the orthodox literature, by orthodox expositions of theory, by orthodox speculation, and by orthodox experiments disclosing orthodox novelty.

This prevailing orthodoxy is as it should be. So far as this orthodox expression has been systematized for the successful evocation of types of aesthetic experience, and the successful indication of the structural interrelations of experience, and the successful demonstration of that structure—so far as this is accomplished, there is truth. We have argued that there is an inherent vagueness in the meanings employed and in the conformities reached. Thus the word "orthodoxy" has been employed to denote the vague, imperfect rightness of our formularized knowledge at any moment. Our knowledge and our skills are limited, and in the nature of things there is infinitude ever pressing new details into some clarity of discrimination.

Because of this imperfection, learned orthodoxy does well to ally itself where reason is playing some part in determining the patterns of occurrence. Orthodoxy can provide the controlled experiment. But here we pass to that partial control where some relevance is secured, but no detail of happenings. Such contact is gained by the absorption into the university of those schools of vocational training for which systematized understanding has importance. There are the professional schools which should fuse closely with the more theoretical side of university work. At present, their chief examples are the schools of Law, Religion, Medicine, Business, Art, Education, Governmental Activities, Engineering. The essential character of these schools is that they study the control of the practice of life by the doctrines of orthodoxy.

The main advantage to a university of this fusion of vocational schools with the central core of theoretical consideration is the increase of suggestiveness. The orthodoxy of reigning theories is a constant menace. By fusion with the schools the area of useful suggestiveness is doubled. It now has two sources. There is the suggestiveness of the vagrant intellect as it contemplates the orthodox expositions and the orthodox types of experiment. This is the suggestiveness of learning. But there is another suggestiveness derived from brute fact. Lawyers are faced with brute fact fitting into no existing legal classification. Religious experiences retain an insistent individuality. Each patient is a unique fact for a doctor. Business requires for its understanding the whole complexity of human motives, and as yet has only been studied from the narrow ledge of economics. Also Art, Education, and Governmental Activities are gold mines of suggestion. It is midsummer madness on the part of universities to withdraw themselves from the closest contact with vocational practices.

Curiously, the withdrawal of universities from the close association with the practice of life is modern. It culminated in the eighteenth and nineteenth centuries, and heralds the decay of a cultural epoch.

I am not talking of the theories that men may have held at any time as to university functions. The point is as to the closeness of the relationship of the universities to the life around them—a closeness so natural as hardly to enter consciousness. In the first place, the universities arose out of nature, and were not exotic constructions imposed from above. The Papacy found universities; it did not devise them. Second, in studying the past we must distinguish between social barriers, trade secrets, and cultural doctrines.

In ancient Greece, whatever occupied a free citizen was worth study. That is why Socrates made himself a nuisance by cross-questioning people in the market place. He discovered the vagueness on which we have been insisting. Many things were done by slaves according to traditional methods. Nobody thought of lightening their labor; first, because it did not matter, and second, because there was no foreknowledge of the penetrating possibilities of modern science. Thus slave labor was a matter of course, without interest. But this is a social barrier, and not a doctrine of cultural activity. In the same way for the serfs of the Middle Ages. But here we must never forget the Benedictine monasteries and the variety of activities housed therein. Also the divine Plato was interested in drinking parties, and in the dances suitable for old gentlemen.

In a modern university the natural place for Aristotle would be somewhere between the Medical School, the Biological Departments, and the School of Education. But as life went on he would have looked in elsewhere. As to Plato, his two longest discourses are on political theory, the longer of the two being intensely practical. Also he made two long and dangerous journeys to give practical advice to governing people. His immediate pupils imitated his example. The Washington "brain trust" is not an American invention.

In the many centuries between Greece and our own times, the direct interplay between universities and practical affairs has been continuous. Salerno, Bologna, Paris, Edinburgh, and the Oxford of Jowett at once come to mind. In fact, almost any university with any length of history before the eighteenth century tells the same tale. And as to men, it suffices to mention Erasmus, Locke, and Newton, among a thousand others. The gross misunderstanding on this point arises from obliviousness of the part played by the great religious institutions, especially in the Middle Ages. They were concerned with action, emotion, and thought. They coordinated intimacies of human feeling. The men directing their activities permeated universities and active life, the same men passing from one to the other of the two spheres. The rapid penetration by the mendicant orders into universities illustrates this point. The survival power of the great religious confederation demonstrates some large conformity of their procedures to the structure of human experience.

For a thousand years the Catholic Church was the deepest influence in the seats of learning and in the social relations of mankind. The mediaeval universities were in touch with the life around them with a direct intimacy denied to their modern descendants. Of course, a large recasting of thought and doctrine was required. The first result was the brilliance of the seventeenth century. But household renovations are dangerous. For universities, the final result has been their seclusion from the variety of human feeling. To-day the activities of the mediaeval churchmen are best represented by the whole bundle of vocational activities, including those of the various churches. In modern life, men of science are the nearest analogues to the mediaeval clergy.

The mediaeval clergy and the cultural humanism of the Hellenic world survive. Science (the search for order realized in nature), Hellenism (the search for value realized in human nature), Religion (the search for value basic for all things), express three factors belonging to the perfection of human nature. They can be studied apart. But they must be lived together in the one life of the individual. Thus there is a tidal law in the emphasis of epochs. At low tide factors are studied primarily in isolation. There is progress with manageable problems. The issue is trivialization; for meaning evaporates.

Importance belongs to the one life of the one individual. This is the doctrine of the platonic soul. At the high tide, combinations of factors dawn on consciousness with the importance of vivid shadows of this full unity of experience. And the knowledge in the low tide has required the high tide to provide compositions as material for thought.

VII

A university should be, at one and the same time, local, national, and world-wide. It is of the essence of learning that it be world-wide, and effectiveness requires local and national adaptations. It is not easy to hold the balance. But unless this difficult balance be held with some genius, the university is to that extent defective.

New England provides the near environment for Harvard, and from that local environment the institution derives its marked individuality, which is its strength. Also the most direct mission for Harvard is to serve the whole of these United States. The maintenance of a great civilization on this continent, from ocean to ocean, is the first purpose of American university life.

But the ideal of the good life, which is civilization—the ideal of a university—is the discovery, the understanding, and the exposition, of the possible harmony of diverse things, involving and exciting every mode of human experience. Thus it is the peculiar function of a university to be an agent of unification. This does not mean the suppression of all but one. With this ideal before it, the notion of bare suppression sends a shiver through the academic framework. It savors of treason. Even local limitations are but means to the highest of all ends. Even methods are limitations. The difficulty is to find a method for the transcendence of methods. The living spirit of a university should exhibit some approach to this transcendence of limits.

The pursuit of harmony has its own difficulties, alike in the realm of action and in the realm of understanding and in the realm of aesthetic enjoyment. The ideal of final harmony lies beyond the reach of human beings. Thus any civilized culture exhibits a mixture of harmony and discord. The university is struggling with discord in its journey toward harmony. It is spreading the enjoyment of such harmonies as the human tradition at that moment conveys, and it is pioneering in the prairies of disordered experience.

When all has been said, the universe is without bounds, learning is world-wide, and the springs of emotion lie below conventionalities. You cannot limit the sources of a great civilization; nor can you assign the stretch of its influence.

To-day Harvard is the greatest of existing cultural institutions. The opportunity is analogous to that of Greece after Marathon, to that of Rome in the reign of Augustus, to that of Christian institutions amid the decay of civilization. Each of these examples recalls tragic failure. But in each there is success which has secured enrichment of human life. If Greece had never been, if Augustan Rome had never been, if Institutional Christianity had never been, if the University of Paris had never been, human life would now be functioning on a lower level, nearer to its animal origins. Will Harvard rise to its opportunity, and in the modern world repeat the brilliant leadership of mediaeval Paris?

IX

Historical Changes

THE Emancipation of Women is inseparably connected with the development of social relations in this country. It is one of the great contributions of the American Republic to the life of mankind. England followed closely and supplied one great thinker who may rank as the intellectual founder of the modern phases of the movement. I mean John Stuart Mill, whose name should never be forgotten in these celebrations.

Those of us who, either by verbal tradition from a previous generation or by the relevant literature, can recall the prevalent tone of thought and of habit belonging to the earlier portion of the nineteenth century in Europe must do homage to the founders whom today we are honoring. They possessed courage and insight. They saw truly that the key of this great emancipation was education, and they acted with complete fearlessness.

Within this period change has not been confined to the emancipation of women. We live in a world of faster and faster transformation. An ancient sage has said, "No one crosses the same river twice." We can apply this saying to our own case: no one lectures to the same students twice; no one lectures on the same subject twice. The flux of the world has assumed a new relation to the spans and the period of human life.

As we think, we live. The mind is the crucible in which we fashion our purposes. The business of universities is the guidance of thought, its content of knowledge, its aesthetic apprehensions, and its activity of criticism.

We must not conceive the mentality of men as their private act of internal self-development. This private aspect of culture has been stressed far too strongly. The key to the history of mankind lies in this fact—as we think, we live.

Culture is the knowledge of the best that has been said and done, according to a famous definition of it. But such conceptions of culture, though true enough as far as they go, are defective. They are too static. They share the whole defect of the Renaissance movement upon which the ideals of the past four centuries have been founded. That movement conceived itself as the recovery of the models of a past civilization. It was based upon the notion of imitation.

Now there is great truth in this notion of culture. It always involves an imitation of the best that has been said and done. Yet something essential has been omitted in this characterization. That "something" is the profound flux of the world.

When knowledge of the distant past was more dim and the pace of change was slower, it was permissible to conceive the flux of the world as a turbulence of details amid an overpowering identity of principles. The changes were minor, the permanences were major.

To-day, this balance as between change and permanence has been decisively altered in two ways.

First, on a grand scale our cosmology discloses a process of overpowering change, from nebulae to stars, from stars to planets, from inorganic matter to life, from life to reason and moral responsibility. We can no longer conceive of existence under the metaphor of a permanent depth of ocean with its surface faintly troubled by transient waves. There is an urge in things which carries the world far beyond its ancient conditions.

Secondly, on the small scale of the individual lives of men, the change in the conditions of social existence is recognizable within the life of one human being and almost within the span of one year.

It is natural at this point to remember Professor Lowes' analysis of Coleridge's poetic conception of life in Xanadu. In that ideal country, it seems that hopes and fears and actions were greatly influenced by "ancestral voices prophesying." Now I suggest to you that today in America "ancestral voices prophesying" are somewhat irrelevant. And for this reason: they do not know what they are talking about. The fact is that our honored ancestors were largely ignorant of modern conditions, and so their prophecies are impressive, vaguely disturbing, but very unpractical.

I have been placing in sharp contrast two antithetical truths, one that culture is assimilation and imitation of what is best in the past, and the other that the transcience of conditions renders the details of the past irrelevant to the present. The problem of modern education is contained in this antithesis.

It is the problem of the understanding of "history" in the greatest sense of that word. In so far as we fail in the education of youth—and of course we do fail—it is because we have not implanted in our students a right conception of their relation to their inheritance from the past. Almost all intellectual knowledge is derived from the past; our mental outfit consists of "ancestral voices prophesying." The criticism of knowledge is the criticism of the past. Whatever be the subject which we teach, our main task is to inculcate how to inherit, appreciatively and critically. What our students should learn is how to face the future with the aid of the past.

Knowledge is the reminiscence by the individual of the experience of the race. But reminiscence is never simple reproduction. The present reacts upon the past. It selects, it emphasizes, it adds. The additions are the new ideas by means of which the life of the present reflects itself upon the past.

Thus culture, besides involving a criticism of tradition, also requires a critical appreciation of novelty. A sane culture is not chiefly concerned with true or false, right or wrong, acceptance or rejection. These are crude extremes betokening a poor appreciation of the complexity of the world.

A new idea has its origin in explicit consciousness by reason of some relevance to the immediate situation. The first task is to appreciate the reason for its origin. What are the factors, logical, emotional, purposeful, or of direct novel perception, which have led to its appearance and its prevalence?

The next task is to define the proper importance of the novelty, to fix its status in the system of thought, and to determine its applications and its limitations in the sphere of action. We have to reduce the idea to its true proportions, and at the same time to express its importance within those proportions.

In respect to our reactions to novelty we are still living in the ancient Ages of Faith. "What went ye out into the wilderness to see? A reed shaken by the wind?"

Thanks to the labors of the eighteenth century, we have inherited an efficient system for the criticism of traditional thought. But in regard to novelty our critical apparatus is only half developed. Each generation runs into childish extremes. Today we adore, and tomorrow we will flog, the images of our saints or at least desert their shrines.

This defect in our culture will never be remedied till we have discovered how to make the great secret of history effective in our way of understanding things. As yet we, who teach, cannot do it. This secret in the history of man is that every idea once was new, and for that reason was then vague, ill-defined, with glorious possibilities or with hideous consequences.

That "two and two make four" was once new and too abstract for importance. That "Caesar should be murdered" was once a secret conjecture, and that "he had been murdered" was once a rumor. We treat the past merely as material for dissection, something settled and obvious, and we have no intimate feeling for the wavering steps of its advance. That "Caesar is murdered" becomes merely an item in the abstract analysis of abstract history. Until mankind understands its own history, intimately as a concrete passage into an unknown future, our culture will never be adequate. We treat our novelties of today as though it were a novel fact that there should be novelty.

History is the drama of effort. The full understanding of it requires an insight into human toiling after its aim. In the absence of some common direction of aim adequately magnificent, there can be no history. The spectacle is then mere chaos.

The drama consists in the mixture of happiness and despair, of failure and victory, arising from the development of human purposes. It includes a tragedy and a comedy. But, as the Athenians well knew, no one is prepared for the relief of comedy until his passions have been purified by the tragic intensity. Comedy is the back-lash of tragedy, making life possible.

The drama of history is more than humor. It discloses an ultimate character in the nature of things, effecting a discrimination of human effort.

It is an easy sophism to dismiss the whole topic of this discussion with the saying that we should concentrate on the future and not on the past; that we want a forward-looking population. This is certainly true. But we cannot get rid of the past quite so easily. For if the past be irrelevant to the present, then the present and the understanding of it go together with the relevance of present to future. It is the business of a sound education to strengthen this sense of derivations and of consequences, and to provide it with understanding.

A weak spot in educational methods is here touched upon. We want an historical background, and even history itself fails to provide it in the required way. We want to get at the facts in the concrete, with their massive background of immediate life. History is apt to present us with the facts in the abstract, detached incidental curiosities. For example, mere lists of presidents of the United States and of Roman emperors are facts in the abstract.

Now every subject of study should be presented as in the abstract and in the concrete. Both sides are wanted. We learn them in the abstract, we feel them in the concrete. Every incident calls a halt in the flux of the world for the sake of its own massive immediate enjoyment. At the same time, it is to be conceived as a moment in the transition of form out of the past into the future.

For example, consider the jubilee which we are celebrating. Fifty years ago women did not go to college, today they do. This is a fact in the abstract, capable of clear statement in a short sentence. But the understanding of the difference in human life, now and fifty years ago, involved in this statement is the comprehension of the fact in the concrete. Still more concrete is the grasp of the mixture of waywardness and inevitableness with which the transition developed—an inevitableness which yet requires the commanding figures round which the drama revolves. The reason of all such celebrations, is the desire to make the past live, to turn abstract knowledge into the concrete feeling.

The function of art is to turn the abstract into the concrete and the concrete into the abstract. It elicits the abstract form from the concrete marble. Education, in every branch of study and in every lecture, is an art. The emphasis may be more on the abstract or more on the concrete. But always there remains the inescapable problem of marriage of form to matter.

Life is short and Art is long. We all fail in our efforts to present the essentials of culture to our students. It remains for their genius to convert our failure into success.

I discern decisive signs of the coming of a new epoch in American thought. The iconoclastic impulse which is so prominent in the literary school today has done its work. It is not rejected. It is not shocking anybody. But its preoccupations have ceased to interest the creative ability under thirty, still more that under twenty-five years of age. The struggle of elderly propriety with middle-aged destructive vehemence is an amusing spectacle to the young. But it has no message for them: it stirs them with no trumpet call.

Their interest is more directly aesthetic and constructive. They are concerned with the beauty derived from artistic finish of workmanship, with style, with restraint, with balance. They seek the play of rapiers, in preference to the blows of sledge hammers.

But they are not mainly critical. Their criticism is a subsidiary moment in their passage towards construction. Their effort after style is also, in like manner, subsidiary. They want to build an edifice of thought which shall also be an edifice of beauty. Every variety of beauty claims their interest—the logical beauty of scientific thought, the beauty to be perceived by the senses, and the beauty of conduct.

In one word, as you will already have seen, the young of today are Athenian, in a sense in which no one belonging to the nineteenth century, either in England or America, was Athenian. In this characterization I am referring, of course, to the few, and not to the many. Perhaps the movement will never attain to widespread influence. It may fail in the luck of throwing up one or two personalities of commanding power. But the trend of interest is certainly there.

You will not misunderstand me. Among the young people of to-day there is no one individual who satisfies, even approximately, the many-sided Athenian ideal which I have sketched. But, as you will remember, in Athens itself there was no person who rose to the full ideal of the typical Athenian. Plato knew well that the ideal of a type is never incarnate in this dusty world. Here again we meet, in a wider sense, the notion of "imitation." It was Plato's phrase for the aim of individuals at the perfection of their type. We have already encountered it as implicit in Arnold's conception of culture.

In one sense an inflexible determinism reigns in this world. For the making of an epoch is already settled by the ideal which its youth set before themselves for imitation. As we think, we live.

In the shaping of this ideal, past and future fuse together in the present. The past is there as an inescapable fact, with its secret impress of modes of operation. In order to conjecture the boundary of possibility we must scan the past.

The pathway of mankind through history has been made visible to our understanding, in fact and in allegory, by that stream of immigrants who in ships across the ocean and in covered wagons across the prairies pursued the lure of their hopes to enlarge the boundaries of life.

They toiled forward, enjoying the stretch of their faculties, hunting, ploughing, starving, thirsting, dying. In this greatest story of the human race the heroism of women attained its utmost height.

X

Universities and Their Function

I

THE expansion of universities is one marked feature of the social life in the present age. All countries have shared in this movement, but more especially America, which thereby occupies a position of honor. It is, however, possible to be overwhelmed even by the gifts of good fortune; and this growth of universities, in number of institutions, in size, and in internal complexity of organization, discloses some danger of destroying the very sources of their usefulness, in the absence of a widespread understanding of the primary functions which universities should perform in the service of a nation. These remarks, as to the necessity for reconsideration of the function of universities, apply to all the more developed countries. They are only more especially applicable to America, because this country has taken the lead in a development which, under wise guidance, may prove to be one of the most fortunate forward steps which civilisation has yet taken.

This article will only deal with the most general principles, though the special problems of the various departments in any university are, of course, innumerable. But generalities require illustration, and for this purpose I choose the business school of a university. This choice is dictated by the fact that business schools represent one of the newer developments of university activity. They are also more particularly relevant to the dominant social activities of modern nations, and for that reason are good examples of the way in which the national life should be affected by the activities of its universities. Also at Harvard, where I have the honour to hold office, the new foundation of a business school on a scale amounting to magnificence has just reached its completion.

There is a certain novelty in the provision of such a school of training, on this scale of magnitude, in one of the few leading universities of the world. It marks the culmination of a movement which for many years past has introduced analogous departments throughout American universities. This is a new fact in the university world; and it alone would justify some general reflections upon the purpose of a university education, and upon the proved importance of that purpose for the welfare of the social organism.

The novelty of business schools must not be exaggerated. At no time have universities been restricted to pure abstract learning. The University of Salerno in Italy, the earliest of European universities, was devoted to medicine. In England, at Cambridge, in the year 1316, a college was founded for the special purpose of providing "clerks for the King's service." Universities have trained clergy, medical men, lawyers, engineers. Business is now a highly intellectualized vocation, so it well fits into the series. There is, however, this novelty: the curriculum suitable for a business school, and the various modes of activity of such a school, are still in the experimental stage. Hence the peculiar importance of recurrence to general principles in connection with the moulding of these schools. It would, however, be an act of presumption on my part if I were to enter upon any consideration of details, or even upon types of policy affecting the balance of the whole training. Upon such questions I have no special knowledge, and therefore have no word of advice.

II

The universities are schools of education, and schools of research. But the primary reason for their existence is not to be found either in the mere knowledge conveyed to the students or in the mere opportunities for research afforded to the members of the faculty.

Both these functions could be performed at a cheaper rate, apart from these very expensive institutions. Books are cheap, and the system of apprenticeship is well understood. So far as the mere imparting of information is concerned, no university has had any justification for existence since the popularisation of printing in the fifteenth century. Yet the chief impetus to the foundation of universities came after that date, and in more recent times has even increased.

The justification for a university is that it preserves the connection between knowledge and the zest of life, by uniting the young and the old in the imaginative consideration of learning. The university imparts information, but it imparts it imaginatively. At least, this is the function which it should perform for society. A university which fails in this respect has no reason for existence. This atmosphere of excitement, arising from imaginative consideration, transforms knowledge. A fact is no longer a bare fact: it is invested with all its possibilities. It is no longer a burden on the memory: it is energising as the poet of our dreams, and as the architect of our purposes.

Imagination is not to be divorced from the facts: it is a way of illuminating the facts. It works by eliciting the general principles which apply to the facts, as they exist, and then by an intellectual survey of alternative possibilities which are consistent with those principles. It enables men to construct an intellectual vision of a new world, and it preserves the zest of life by the suggestion of satisfying purposes.

Youth is imaginative, and if the imagination be strengthened by discipline this energy of imagination can in great measure be preserved through life. The tragedy of the world is that those who are imaginative have but slight experience, and those who are experienced have feeble imaginations. Fools act on imagination without knowledge; pedants act on knowledge without imagination. The task of a university is to weld together imagination and experience.

The initial discipline of imagination in its period of youthful vigour requires that there be no responsibility for immediate action. The habit of unbiased thought, whereby the ideal variety of exemplifications is discerned in its derivation from general principles, cannot be acquired when there is the daily task of preserving a concrete organisation. You must be free to think rightly and wrongly, and free to appreciate the variousness of the universe undisturbed by its perils.

These reflections upon the general functions of a university can be at once translated in terms of the particular functions of a business school. We need not flinch from the assertion that the main function of such a school is to produce men with a greater zest for business. It is a libel upon human nature to conceive that zest for life is the product of pedestrian purposes directed toward the narrow routine of material comforts. Mankind by its pioneering instinct, and in a hundred other ways, proclaims the falsehood of that lie.

In the modern complex social organism, the adventure of life cannot be disjoined from intellectual adventure. Amid simpler circumstances, the pioneer can follow the urge of his instinct, directed toward the scene of his vision from the mountain top. But in the complex organisations of modern business the intellectual adventure of analysis, and of imaginative reconstruction, must precede any successful reorganisation. In a simpler world, business relations were simpler, being based on the immediate contact of man with man and on immediate confrontation with all relevant material circumstances. To-day business organisation requires an imaginative grasp of the psychologies of populations engaged in differing modes of occupation; of populations scattered through cities, through mountains, through plains; of populations on the ocean, and of populations in mines, and of populations in forests. It requires an imaginative grasp of conditions in the tropics, and of conditions in temperate zones. It requires an imaginative grasp of the interlocking interests of great organisations, and of the reactions of the whole complex to any change in one of its elements. It requires an imaginative understanding of laws of political economy, not merely in the abstract, but also with the power to construe them in terms of the particular circumstances of a concrete business. It requires some knowledge of the habits of government, and of the variations of those habits under diverse conditions. It requires an imaginative vision of the binding forces of any human organisation, a sympathetic vision of the limits of human nature and of the conditions which evoke loyalty of service. It requires some knowledge of the laws of health, and of the laws of fatigue, and of the conditions for sustained reliability. It requires an imaginative understanding of the social effects of the conditions of factories. It requires a sufficient conception of the role of applied science in modern society. It requires that discipline of character which can say "yes" and "no" to other men, not by reason of blind obstinacy, but with firmness derived from a conscious evaluation of relevant alternatives.

The universities have trained the intellectual pioneers of our civilisation—the priests, the lawyers, the statesmen, the doctors, the men of science, and the men of letters. They have been the home of those ideals which lead men to confront the confusion of their present times. The Pilgrim Fathers left England to found a state of society according to the ideals of their religious faith; and one of their earlier acts was the foundation of Harvard University in Cambridge, named after that ancient mother of ideals in England, to which so many of them owed their training. The conduct of business now requires intellectual imagination of the same type as that which in former times has mainly passed into those other occupations; and the universities are the organisations which have supplied this type of mentality for the service of the progress of the European races.

In early mediaeval history the origin of universities was obscure and almost unnoticed. They were a gradual and natural growth. But their existence is the reason for the sustained, rapid progressiveness of European life in so many fields of activity. By their agency the adventure of action met the adventure of thought. It would not have been possible antecedently to have divined that such organisations would have been successful. Even now, amid the imperfections of all things human, it is sometimes difficult to understand how they succeed in their work. Of course there is much failure in the work of universities. But, if we take a broad view of history, their success has been remarkable and almost uniform. The cultural histories of Italy, of France, of Germany, of Holland, of Scotland, of England, of the United States, bear witness to the influence of universities. By "cultural history" I am not chiefly thinking of the lives of scholars; I mean the energising of the lives of those men who gave to France, to Germany, and to other countries that impress of types of human achievement which, by their addition to the zest of life, form the foundation of our patriotism. We love to be members of a society which can do those things.

There is one great difficulty which hampers all the higher types of human endeavor. In modern times this difficulty has even increased in its possibilities for evil. In any large organisation the younger men, who are novices, must be set to jobs which consist in carrying out fixed duties in obedience to orders. No president of a large corporation meets his youngest employee at his office door with the offer of the most responsible job which the work of that corporation includes. The young men are set to work at a fixed routine, and only occasionally even see the president as he passes in and out of the building. Such work is a great discipline. It imparts knowledge, and it produces reliability of character; also it is the only work for which the young men, in that novice stage, are fit, and it is the work for which they are hired. There can be no criticism of the custom, but there may be an unfortunate effect—prolonged routine work dulls the imagination.

The result is that qualities essential at a later stage of a career are apt to be stamped out in an earlier stage. This is only an instance of the more general fact, that necessary technical excellence can only be acquired by a training which is apt to damage those energies of mind which should direct the technical skill. This is the key fact in education, and the reason for most of its difficulties.

The way in which a university should function in the preparation for an intellectual career, such as modern business or one of the older professions, is by promoting the imaginative consideration of the various general principles underlying that career. Its students thus pass into their period of technical apprenticeship with their imaginations already practised in connecting details with general principles. The routine then receives its meaning, and also illuminates the principles which give it that meaning. Hence, instead of a drudgery issuing in a blind rule of thumb, the properly trained man has some hope of obtaining an imagination disciplined by detailed facts and by necessary habits.

Thus the proper function of a university is the imaginative acquisition of knowledge. Apart from this importance of the imagination, there is no reason why business men, and other professional men, should not pick up their facts bit by bit as they want them for particular occasions. A university is imaginative or it is nothing—at least nothing useful.

III

Imagination is a contagious disease. It cannot be measured by the yard, or weighed by the pound, and then delivered to the students by members of the faculty. It can only be communicated by a faculty whose members themselves wear their learning with imagination. In saying this, I am only repeating one of the oldest of observations. More than two thousand years ago the ancients symbolised learning by a torch passing from hand to hand down the generations. That lighted torch is the imagination of which I speak. The whole art in the organisation of a university is the provision of a faculty whose learning is lighted up with imagination. This is the problem of problems in university education; and unless we are careful the recent vast extension of universities in number of students and in variety of activities—of which we are so justly proud—will fail in producing its proper results, by the mishandling of this problem.

The combination of imagination and learning normally requires some leisure, freedom from restraint, freedom from harassing worry, some variety of experiences, and the stimulation of other minds diverse in opinion and diverse in equipment. Also there is required the excitement of curiosity, and the self-confidence derived from pride in the achievements of the surrounding society in procuring the advance of knowledge. Imagination cannot be acquired once and for all, and then kept indefinitely in an ice box to be produced periodically in stated quantities. The learned and imaginative life is a way of living, and is not an article of commerce.

It is in respect to the provision and utilisation of these conditions for an efficient faculty that the two functions of education and research meet together in a university. Do you want your teachers to be imaginative? Then encourage them to research. Do you want your researchers to be imaginative? Then bring them into intellectual sympathy with the young at the most eager, imaginative period of life, when intellects are just entering upon their mature discipline. Make your researchers explain themselves to active minds, plastic and with the world before them; make your young students crown their period of intellecual acquisition by some contact with minds gifted with experience of intellectual adventure. Education is discipline for the adventure of life; research is intellectual adventure; and the universities should be homes of adventure shared in common by young and old. For successful education there must always be a certain freshness in the knowledge dealt with. It must either be new in itself or it must be invested with some novelty of application to the new world of new times. Knowledge does not keep any better than fish. You may be dealing with knowledge of the old species, with some old truth; but somehow or other it must come to the students, as it were, just drawn out of the sea and with the freshness of its immediate importance.

It is the function of the scholar to evoke into life wisdom and beauty which, apart from his magic, would remain lost in the past. A progressive society depends upon its inclusion of three groups —scholars, discoverers, inventors. Its progress also depends upon the fact that its educated masses are composed of members each with a tinge of scholarship, a tinge of discovery, and a tinge of invention. I am here using the term "discovery" to mean the progress of knowledge in respect to truths of some high generality, and the term "invention" to mean the progress of knowledge in respect to the application of general truths in particular ways subservient to present needs. It is evident that these three groups merge into each other, and also that men engaged in practical affairs are properly to be called inventors so far as they contribute to the progress of society. But any one individual has his own limitation of function, and his own peculiar needs. What is important for a nation is that there shall be a very close relation between all types of its progressive elements, so that the study may influence the market place, and the market place the study. Universities are the chief agencies for this fusion of progressive activities into an effective instrument of progress. Of course they are not the only agencies, but it is a fact that to-day the progressive nations are those in which universities flourish.

It must not be supposed that the output of a university in the form of original ideas is solely to be measured by printed papers and books labeled with the names of their authors. Mankind is as individual in its mode of output as in the substance of its thoughts. For some of the most fertile minds composition in writing, or in a form reducible to writing, seems to be an impossibility. In every faculty you will find that some of the more brilliant teachers are not among those who publish. Their originality requires for its expression direct intercourse with their pupils in the form of lectures, or of personal discussion. Such men exercise an immense influence; and yet, after the generation of their pupils has passed away, they sleep among the innumerable unthanked benefactors of humanity. Fortunately, one of them is immortal—Socrates.

Thus it would be the greatest mistake to estimate the value of each member of a faculty by the printed work signed with his name. There is at the present day some tendency to fall into this error; and an emphatic protest is necessary against an attitude on the part of authorities which is damaging to efficiency and unjust to unselfish zeal.

But, when all such allowances have been made, one good test for the general efficiency of a faculty is that as a whole it shall be producing in published form its quota of contributions of thought. Such a contribution is to be estimated in weight of thought, and not in number of words.

This survey shows that the management of a university faculty has no analogy to that of a business organisation. The public opinion of the faculty, and a common zeal for the purposes of the university, form the only effective safeguards for the high level of university work. The faculty should be a band of scholars, stimulating each other, and freely determining their various activities. You can secure certain formal requirements, that lectures are given at stated times and that instructors and students are in attendance. But the heart of the matter lies beyond all regulation.

The question of justice to the teachers has very little to do with the case. It is perfectly just to hire a man to perform any legal services under any legal conditions as to times and salary. No one need accept the post unless he so desires.

The sole question is, What sort of conditions will produce the type of faculty which will run a successful university? The danger is that it is quite easy to produce a faculty entirely unfit— a faculty of very efficient pedants and dullards. The general public will only detect the difference after the university has stunted the promise of youth for scores of years.

The modern university system in the great democratic countries will only be successful if the ultimate authorities exercise singular restraint, so as to remember that universities cannot be dealt with according to the rules and policies which apply to the familiar business corporations. Business schools are no exception to this law of university life. There is really nothing to add to what the presidents of many American universities have recently said in public on this topic. But whether the effective portion of the general public, in America or other countries, will follow their advice appears to be doubtful. The whole point of a university, on its educational side, is to bring the young under the intellectual influence of a band of imaginative scholars. There can be no escape from proper attention to the conditions which—as experience has shown—will produce such a band.

IV

The two premier universities of Europe, in age and in dignity, are the University of Paris and the University of Oxford. I will speak of my own country because I know it best. The University of Oxford may have sinned in many ways. But, for all her deficiencies, she has throughout the ages preserved one supreme merit, beside which all failures in detail are as dust in the balance: for century after century, throughout the long course of her existence, she has produced bands of scholars who treated learning imaginatively. For that service alone, no one who loves culture can think of her without emotion.

But it is quite unnecessary for me to cross the ocean for my examples. The author of the Declaration of Independence, Mr. Jefferson, has some claim to be the greatest American. The perfection of his various achievements certainly places him among the few great men of all ages. He founded a university, and devoted one side of his complex genius to placing that university amid every circumstance which could stimulate the imagination —beauty of buildings, of situation, and every other stimulation of equipment and organization.

There are many other universities in America which can point my moral, but my final example shall be Harvard—the representative university of the Puritan movement. The New England Puritans of the seventeenth and eighteenth centuries were the most intensely imaginative people, restrained in their outward expression, and fearful of symbolism by physical beauty, but, as it were, racked with the intensity of spiritual truths intellectually imagined. The Puritan faculties of those centuries must have been imaginative indeed, and they produced great men whose names have gone round the world. In later times Puritanism softened, and, in the golden age of literary New England, Emerson, Lowell, and Longfellow set their mark upon Harvard. The modern scientific age then gradually supervenes, and again in William James we find the typical imaginative scholar.

To-day business comes to Harvard; and the gift which the University has to offer is the old one of imagination, the lighted torch which passes from hand to hand. It is a dangerous gift, which has started many a conflagration. If we are timid as to that danger, the proper course is to shut down our universities. Imagination is a gift which has often been associated with great commercial peoples—with Greece, with Florence, with Venice, with the learning of Holland, and with the poetry of England. Commerce and imagination thrive together. It is a gift which all must pray for their country who desire for it that abiding greatness achieved by Athens:

> Her citizens, imperial spirits,
> Rule the present from the past.

For American education no smaller ideal can suffice.

Selected Bibliography

THE MEANING OF CIVILIZATION

GOHEEN, J., "Whitehead's Theory of Value," in *The Philosophy of Alfred North Whitehead*. P. A. Schilpp, Ed. Evanston, Northwestern University Press, 1941.

HOOPER, S. E., "A Reasonable Theory of Morality" (Alexander and Whitehead). *Philosophy*, Vol. XXV, 1950, pp. 54–67.

JOHNSON, A. H., " 'Truth, Beauty, and Goodness' in the Philosophy of A. N. Whitehead." *Philosophy of Science*, Vol. XI, 1944, pp. 9–29.

———, "Whitehead's Philosophy of Civilization," in *Whitehead and the Modern World*. Boston, Beacon Press, 1950, pp. 42–54.

———, *Whitehead's Philosophy of Civilization*. Boston, Beacon Press, 1958, Chapter 1.

MORGAN, G. JR., "Whitehead's Theory of Value." *International Journal of Ethics*, Vol. XLVII, 1936–37, pp. 308–316.

MORRIS, B., "The Art-process and the Aesthetic Factor in Whitehead's Philosophy," in *The Philosophy of Alfred North Whitehead*. P. A. Schilpp, Ed. Evanston, Northwestern University Press, 1941.

SCHILPP, P. A., "Whitehead's Theory of Value," in *The Philosophy of Alfred North Whitehead*. P. A. Schilpp, Ed. Evanston, Northwestern University Press, 1941.

DECISIVE SOCIAL FACTORS

JOHNSON, A. H., *Whitehead's Philosophy of Civilization*. Boston, Beacon Press, 1958, Chapter 2.

———, "Whitehead's Philosophy of History." *Journal of the History of Ideas*, Vol. VII, 1946, pp. 234–249.

SWABEY, M. C., *The Judgment of History*. New York, Philosophical Library, 1954, pp. 205–213.

SOCIAL PROBLEMS

BEER, S. H., *The City of Reason*. Cambridge, Harvard University Press, 1949.

JOHNSON, A. H., "The Social Philosophy of Alfred North Whitehead." *The Journal of Philosophy*, Vol. XL, 1943, pp. 261–271.

———, "Whitehead and the Making of Tomorrow." *Philosophy and Phenomenological Research*, Vol. V, 1945, pp. 398–406.

———, *Whitehead's Philosophy of Civilization*. Boston, Beacon Press, 1958, Chapter 4.

WELLS, H. K., "The Philosophy of A. N. Whitehead." *Science and Society*, Vol. XVI, 1951–52, pp. 27–43.

EDUCATION

HOLMES, H. W., "Whitehead's Views on Education," in *The Philosophy of Alfred North Whitehead*. P. A. Schilpp, Ed. Evanston, Northwestern University Press, 1941.

HUTCHINS, R. M., "A Reply to Professor Whitehead." *The Atlantic*, Vol. CLVIII, 1936.

JOHNSON, A. H., "Whitehead's Discussion of Education." *Education*, Vol. LXVI, 1946, pp. 653–671.

———, *Whitehead's Philosophy of Civilization*. Boston, Beacon Press, 1958, Chapter 5.

LEVI, A. W., "The Problem of Higher Education: Whitehead and Hutchins." *Harvard Educational Review*, Vol. VII, 1937.

INDEX

Imagination, 41–42, 188–191, 192–195. *See also* Suggestiveness

Imperialism, 31–35, 112–114, 128–135, 140–142

Individual (respect for), Individualism, 6–7, 64–78, 93–94, 124–126

Isolation, 111–123

Israel, 31–32, 123–124, 126–128, 130–135

Jews, *see* Israel

Material factors, 17–18, 28–29, 59, 106–110, 146–147. *See also* Geography

Mathematics, 39–40, 161–163

Men, 14–17, 27–28, 59, 81–90, 98–99, 102–106, 148–149

Moslem world, 30–32, 54, 122–123, 128–135

Nationalism, *see* America, England, Israel, Moslem world

Novelty, 20, 41–43, 55–61, 63–78, 126, 169, 177–178

Order, 19, 53–56, 125, 167–168, 192

Past, uses of the, 42–43, 62, 92–94, 143, 179–182

Peace, 5, 175

Persuasion, rather than force, 8–9, 130, 133, 139–140. *See also* Imperialism

Philosophy, 11, 169, 192–193, 195. *See also* Plato

Pilgrim fathers (Puritans), 93–94, 110, 191, 198–199

Plato, 38, 160–161, 163–164, 173

Political principles, 20, 29–37, 53–61, 111–143. *See also* Compromise, Cooperation, War

Radcliffe College, 42–43

Religion, 16–17, 125, 174. *See also* Church, the

Russia, 48, 60, 99, 119–123, 141

Scholarship, traditional, 164–166

Science, 59, 68–69, 92, 174. *See also* Evolution, Mathematics

Skepticism, 162, 169, 183

Social forces, decisive, 12–18, 20–21. *See also* Economic factors, Ideas, Men, Material factors

Suggestiveness, 166–167, 171–172

Technical developments, 56–58, 59–60, 72

Tolerance, 7–8, 55, 99, 131, 142–143

Truth, 6, 22, 159. *See also* Clarity, and vagueness, Philosophy

University
application of knowledge, 44–47, 77–78, 169–174, 187–188
education, general discussion of, 41–42, 44, 91–92, 157–176
faculty, 168–169, 193–197

War, 33, 115

Whitehead, life of, vii–ix, 35–37, 79–81, 145–155

Wisdom, *see* Philosophy

Set in Linotype Garamond No. 3
Format by Marguerite Swanton